THE OFFICIAL
IPSWICH TOWN
QUIZ BOOK

THE OFFICIAL IPSWICH TOWN QUIZ BOOK

JOHN DT WHITE

APEX PUBLISHING LTD

First published in 2005 by
Apex Publishing Ltd
PO Box 7086, Clacton on Sea, Essex, CO15 5WN, England

www.apexpublishing.co.uk

Copyright © 2005 by John DT White
The author has asserted his moral rights

British Library Cataloguing-in-Publication Data
A catalogue record for this book
is available from the British Library

ISBN 1-904444-57-1

Typeset in 10.5pt Times New Roman

Production Manager: Chris Cowlin

Cover Design: Andrew Macey

Printed and bound in Great Britain

This book is dedicated to Sir Bobby Robson and the Ipswich Town players who won the UEFA Cup in 1981.

FOREWORD

Welcome to the definitive Ipswich Town Football Club Quiz Book! In the following pages you will find a plethora of quiz questions to test even the most knowledgeable of Town Fans. When asked to write this foreword I requested an advance copy on receipt of which I found myself quickly and totally immersed in the content, testing myself and, all too often, flicking to the back for the answers! I am sure you will enjoy this book as you challenge yourself and friends.

I would like to thank Apex Publishing for agreeing to donate £1.00 for each and every quiz book purchased to our own Ipswich Town Community Trust. As you may know, our Community Trust is now a registered charity in its own right, a subsidiary of the Club but operating with its own distinct Board of Trustees. Its objectives focus on LEARNING, ACTIVE and LIVING being the areas in which we are capitalising on the power of football to stimulate education for those that need extra help, football opportunity for thousands of young people who just want to play the game and a healthy lifestyle, diet and fitness awareness for just about all of us!

So, in buying this book you are not only in for hours of fun but you are also helping the Ipswich Town Community Trust, which plays such a vital part in helping to grow and perpetuate our fan base amongst old and young alike.

Enjoy!

With best wishes.

David Sheepshanks
Ipswich Town Chairman

INTRODUCTION

I am delighted that David Sheepshanks very kindly agreed to write the Foreword to my book and my thanks must also go to all of those people who gave me a quote to use, including Joe Royle, Simon Milton, etc.

However, these people deserve my thanks above all others. Firstly, Chris Cowlin at Apex Publishing Ltd for suggesting the idea and, secondly, I would like to express my sincere thanks to Mike Noye, Alison Holman, Terry Baxter, Kelly Campbell and Anne-Marie Hutchinson, at Ipswich Town Football Club. And last but certainly not least, my sincere thanks must go to Ralph Morris and his website, **www.prideofanglia.com**. Ralph has spent many hours maintaining the most comprehensive website available on Ipswich Town Football Club and deserves much credit for all of his dedication and commitment.

On a personal level I would also like to thank Mike and Ralph for proofreading my work and for pointing out any errors I may have made along the way.

So, I sincerely hope you enjoy my book and hopefully it will bring back many wonderful memories of a glorious past and never to be forgotten moments in the history of Ipswich Town Football Club.

Finally, my thanks must also go to my Janice and our two sons, Marc and Paul, who support everything I do.

John DT White

THE HISTORY - 1

1.   In what year was Ipswich Town formed - 1878, 1879 or 1880?

2.   Against what "United" did Ipswich set their home record attendance on 8th March 1975 in an FA Cup 6th Round tie?

3.   Name the player who holds the record for the most appearances for the club.

4.   How many times have Ipswich won the First Division Championship (now known as the FA Premier League)?

5.   What did the club "do" in 1936?

6.   In what "League" did the club play prior to their election to the Football League?

7.   To the nearest "500", what is the capacity of Portman Road for the 2005-2006 season?

8.   What is the furthest Round the club has progressed to in the League Cup?

9.   Can you name the player who holds the record for the highest transfer fee received by the club?

10. What is the club's best ever League win - 7-0, 8-0 or 9-0?

SEASON 2001-2002

11.   In what position did Ipswich finish in the FA Premier League - 18th, 19th or 20th?

12.   Against what Midlands club did Ipswich record their first League win of the season, a 3-1 home win on 21st August?

13.   What "George" scored twice in the game in Q12?

14.   Can you recall the "United" that beat Ipswich 4-0 on 22 September?

15.   Who scored twice for Ipswich in a 3-2 loss away to Charlton Athletic and in a 2-2 away draw at Newcastle United?

16.   Name either of Ipswich's last 2 League scorers during the 2001-2002 season.

17.   What team won the 2001-2002 FA Premier League?

18.   To the nearest 5, with how many points did Ipswich end the season with?

19.   Can you name the London club that beat Ipswich 3-2 on New Year's Day despite Ipswich scoring in the 1st and 5th minutes?

20.   Name the Lancashire club that beat Ipswich 6-0 at Portman Road and 5-0 on their own ground in the Premiership.

MICK MILLS - 1

21.   In what year did Mick make his Professional debut for Ipswich Town - 1964, 1965 or 1966?

22.   What club did Mick sign for when he left Town?

23.   To the nearest 50, how many League appearances did he make for Town?

24.   From what club did Town sign Mick?

25.   How many full International caps did he win - 42, 52 or 62?

26.   Can you recall the "City" he joined after leaving the team in Q22?

27.   In what year during the early 1980s did he leave Portman Road?

28.   In what year did Mick captain England at the World Cup Finals?

29.   Following on from Q28, who appointed Mick as captain of England?

30.   What "City" was Mick the Caretaker Manager of in October 2001?

TRIVIA - 1

31. Can you recall the "City" Joe Royle signed for when he left Manchester City in 1977?

32. Up to the end of the 2004-2005 season, how many Town players have been sent off against Norwich City - 2, 12 or 22?

33. To what London club did Ipswich lose 2-1 at home on Christmas Day 1951 and 4-0 away on Boxing Day 1951?

34. Who was Town's leading goalscorer during the 2004-2005 season with 20 goals?

35. Name the "Steve" who set a Town record of 175 consecutive appearances for the club during the 1984-1985 season.

36. Can you name the Italian club from which Town signed Jonas Alexdal in 1999?

37. The highest number of consecutive defeats suffered by Town is 10. Can you recall the "City" that beat them twice in this sequence of losses in the space of only 8 days?

38. Name the "Ted" who holds the club record for the highest number of goals scored in a season.

39. What was the first trophy won by the club?

40. Against what South Coast club did Ipswich record their best ever League win, 7-0, on 7 November 1964 in a Division 2 game?

COMINGS AND GOINGS - 1

*ALL YOU HAVE TO DO HERE IS ASSOCIATE THE PLAYER
WITH THE TEAM HE LEFT TO JOIN IPSWICH OR THE TEAM
HE JOINED AFTER LEAVING IPSWICH*

41.	Titus Bramble	to Everton
42.	John Deehan	from Linfield
43.	George Burley	to Glasgow Rangers
44.	Frank Clarke	from Norwich City
45.	Alan Brazil	from Millwall
46.	Paul Goddard	from Queens Park Rangers
47.	Marcus Bent	to Newcastle United
48.	Chris Bart-Williams	to Tottenham Hotspur
49.	Terry Butcher	to Sunderland
50.	Bryan Hamilton	from Charlton Athletic

THE 1980s - 1

51. Name the Town player who won the PFA Players' Player of the Year Award for season 1980-1981.

52. Can you name the London club that defeated Town in the 1st Division/2nd Division Play-Off game in season 1986-1987?

53. Who during the 1983-1984 season became the youngest ever player to play for Ipswich Town aged 16 years and 57 days?

54. Can you name the Town players who finished in 2nd and 3rd place respectively behind John Wark in the 1980-1981 PFA Players' Player of the Year Award?

55. Can you name the Italian side that put Town out of the UEFA Cup in 1982-1983?

56. Name the "Frank" who was voted Town's Player of the Year in season 1987-1988.

57. Can you name the Ipswich player who in season 1988-1989 became the first player from the Soviet Union to play in the Football League?

58. Who was Town's leading goalscorer in both the 1983-1984 and 1984-1985 seasons?

59. In what season did Town lose more than 50% of their League games, resulting in relegation to Division 2?

60. Who was appointed Town's new Manager when Bobby Robson left?

DERBY DAYS: IPSWICH TOWN
v. NORWICH CITY - 1

61.   What Town player has played in the most Derby games?

62.   How many Derby goals did Bryan Hamilton score for Town - 3, 5 or 7?

63.   Can you name the former Town striker who coached City's Under-13s during the 1999-2000 season?

64.   Name the "Mick" who made 4 Derby substitute appearances between 1972 and 1978.

65.   In what "Cup" competition did Town beat City 1-0 after extra time in a 2nd Round game at Portman Road on 20 December 1988?

66.   This goalkeeper played for City from 1993 to 2001 and Town from 2001 to 2004. Name him.

67.   What "Ray" with 8 goals is Town's second highest goalscorer in Derby games?

68.   Can you recall the season in which the first FA Premier League Derby game was played?

69.   Name the former Norwich City and Nottingham Forest striker who had an unsuccessful Trial at Portman Road.

70.   This former City player scored 10 goals in 47 appearances for the Canaries between 1971 and 1975 and later became Town Manager. Who is he?

PLAYERS - 1

71. Name the defender who was voted Ipswich Town's Greatest Player of all time.

72. Can you name the Spanish club from which Town signed Finidi George and which was the same club he re-joined after leaving Town?

73. Who was Ipswich Town's longest serving player at the start of the 2004-2005 season?

74. To the nearest £500,000, how much did Matteo Sereni cost the club?

75. When Lee Chapman left Town in 1996, what Welsh "City" did he join?

76. Can you recall the "Kevin" who finished the 1986-1987 season as Town's leading goalscorer?

77. This "John" played for Norwich City from 1981 to 1986 and then moved to Portman Road where he played for Town up to 1988. Name him.

78. Who made his debut for Ipswich in the UEFA Cup 3rd Preliminary Round against FC Avenir Beggen (Luxembourg) in August 2002 to become the youngest ever Town player to play in Europe?

79. Following on from Q78, can you name the player he came on as a substitute for who had held the same record for less than 1 year?

80.   Name the player who finished the season as the Pool's top goalscorer in both the 1999-2000 and 2000-2001 seasons before he joined Ipswich?

BLUES' PLAYER OF THE YEAR - 1

ALL YOU HAVE TO DO HERE IS ASSOCIATE THE PLAYER WITH THE SEASON HE WAS VOTED THE IPSWICH TOWN PLAYER OF THE YEAR BY THE FANS

81.	2003-2004	Craig Forrest
82.	1999-2000	John Wark
83.	1997-1998	Mick Stockwell
84.	1994-1995	Terry Butcher
85.	1992-1993	Allan Hunter
86.	1989-1990	Kevin Beattie
87.	1985-1986	James Scowcroft
88.	1978-1979	Ian Westlake
89.	1975-1976	Arnold Muhren
90.	1972-1973	Matt Holland

UEFA CUP WINNERS - 1

91.   In what year did Town win the UEFA Cup?

92.   Who captained Ipswich to UEFA Cup success?

93.   What team did Town beat in the UEFA Cup Final?

94.   Can you recall the Greek side Town beat in the 1st Round of the competition?

95.   How many goals did John Wark score in the competition, setting a new record for the highest number of goals scored?

96.   Name the Town defender who scored Ipswich's goal in their 1-0 Semi-Final away win.

97.   What French side did Town beat home and away in the Quarter-Finals?

98.   How many of their away Legs did Ipswich win on their way to claiming the trophy?

99.   Can you name the future Nottingham Forest and Tottenham Hotspur "Johnny" who scored against Town in the Final?

100.   Can you name the future captain of a European Championship winning team that played for the team in Q97?

FINAL LEAGUE POSITIONS - 1

*ALL YOU HAVE TO DO HERE IS ASSOCIATE TOWN WITH
THEIR FINAL POSITION IN THE LEAGUE FOR THE SEASON
MENTIONED (FOR EXAMPLE 1961-1962 Div 1 - ?)*

101.	1961-1962	Div 1	16th
102.	1968-1969	Div 1	7th
103.	1973-1974	Div 1	6th
104.	1978-1979	Div 1	3rd
105.	1982-1983	Div 1	4th
106.	1986-1987	Div 2	1st
107.	1992-1993	Prem	5th
108.	1995-1996	Div 1	9th
109.	1997-1998	Div 1	12th
110.	1999-2000	Div 1	5th

PENALTY SHOOT-OUTS

111.   Up to the end of the 2004-2005 season, how many Penalty Shoot-Outs has Ipswich been involved in - 7, 8 or 9?

112.   Against what "Lokomotive" was Town involved in their first ever competitive Penalty Shoot-Out?

113.   Following on from Q112, can you name any 1 of Town's 3 scorers in the Penalty Shoot-Out?

114.   Of the total number of Penalty Shoot-Outs in Q111, how many did Town win?

115.   What London club has Town met twice in a Penalty Shoot-Out?

116.   Can you name the "Peter" who was the first Town player to miss from the spot in a competitive Penalty Shoot-Out?

117.   Who is the only Ipswich goalkeeper to have been involved in 2 competitive Penalty Shoot-Outs?

118.   Name the Spanish side that beat Town in a Penalty Shoot-Out in the UEFA Cup in 1977.

119.   Can you name the side that put Town out of the Worthington Cup in 2002 after a Penalty Shoot-Out?

120.   Following on from Q119, name any 2 of the 4 Town players who scored from the spot.

SIR ALF RAMSEY - 1

121. In what year was he appointed the Manager of Ipswich Town - 1954, 1955 or 1956?

122. Can you name the seaside "United" Ipswich played against in Alf Ramsey's first game in charge?

123. At what South Coast club did Alf begin his Professional playing career?

124. Name the London club he signed for in 1949.

125. What was the first trophy won by Town under Alf Ramsey's management?

126. In what year did he lead Ipswich to the First Division Championship?

127. In what year did Alf Ramsey become Sir Alf Ramsey?

128. To the nearest 50, for how many games was he in charge of Ipswich Town?

129. What "City" was he appointed the Manager of in 1977?

130. Can you recall the year he was appointed the Manager of the England Football Team?

SIR BOBBY ROBSON

131.   Who did Bobby succeed as England Manager?

132.   To the nearest 5, how many full International caps did he win with England?

133.   In what year did Bobby make his England debut as a player - 1956, 1957 or 1958?

134.   In what year did Bobby manage Town to FA Cup success?

135.   At what London club did Bobby begin his Professional career as a footballer?

136.   Prior to joining the team in Q135, his nearby North East club attempted to sign him as a 15-year-old. Can you name the team?

137.   Can you name the Dutch side Bobby was appointed the Manager of after the 1990 World Cup Finals in Italy?

138.   What Canadian "Whitecaps" gave Bobby his first taste of management in 1967?

139.   At what World Cup Finals did Bobby play for England?

140.   Name the Midlands club, a Premier League club during the 2004-2005 season, that Bobby signed for in March 1956.

TOWN AT THE WORLD CUP FINALS

141. How many Town players played at the 2002 World Cup Finals?

142. Following on from Q141, name any 1 of them.

143. What Town player has played the most games at the World Cup Finals for his country?

144. Can you name the only Ipswich player who played at the 1994 World Cup Finals in the USA?

145. Who was the first Town player to score a goal at the World Cup Finals?

146. At how many different World Cup Final Tournaments has a player from Ipswich Town actually played in the Finals?

147. Name any 4 of the 6 Town players that played at the World Cup Finals in Spain in 1982.

148. Can you name the Town player who has scored the most goals at the Final Stages of the World Cup?

149. Name the Town player who played in 5 World Cup Final games and captained his country in all 5 matches.

150. Can you recall the future World Cup winners against which Paul Mariner scored for England during the 1982 Finals in Bilbao, Spain on 16 June 1982?

SQUAD NUMBERS 2004-2005 - 1

*ALL YOU HAVE TO DO HERE IS ASSOCIATE THE PLAYER
WITH HIS SQUAD NUMBER FOR THE 2004-2005 SEASON*

151.　　Lewis Price　　　　　　　　No. 6

152.　　Jimmy Juan　　　　　　　　No. 21

153.　　Richard Naylor　　　　　　No. 32

154.　　Pablo Counago　　　　　　No. 17

155.　　Ian Westlake　　　　　　　No. 4

156.　　Scott Mitchell　　　　　　No. 34

157.　　Dean Bowditch　　　　　　No. 23

158.　　Jason De Vos　　　　　　　No. 33

159.　　Owen Garvan　　　　　　　No. 9

160.　　Shefki Kuqi　　　　　　　　No. 19

SEASON 2003-2004 - 1

161. What Bulgarian side did Town draw 1-1 with in a pre-season friendly at Portman Road on 1 August 2003?

162. Can you recall the team with the initials "KH" that Town met in the 1st Round of the Carling Cup?

163. Who scored Town's first League goal of the season?

164. Against what team did Town record their first League win of the season?

165. Name the Town player who scored in 3 consecutive games against Crystal Palace, Preston North End and Gillingham.

166. Who was Town's leading goalscorer for the season with 16 goals?

167. Can you name the London side that ended Town's hopes of a return to the Premiership when they lost to them in the Play-Off Semi-Finals?

168. What "City" did Town draw 1-1 with at Portman Road on the last day of the League season?

169. In what position in the League did Town finish?

170. Name the team that beat Town 2-0 at Portman Road and 3-1 at their own ground.

TRIVIA - 2

171. Who succeeded Bobby Ferguson as Manager in season 1987-1988?

172. What occasion was celebrated when Ipswich visited Kettering Town during their successful 1961-1962 Championship winning season?

173. How many times was John Wark sent off while playing for Ipswich - 2, 4 or 6?

174. Up to the end of the 2004-2005 season, what is the highest number of consecutive wins put together by Town - 9, 10 or 11?

175. Can you name the "Trevor" who was voted the Ipswich Town player of the year for season 1983-1984?

176. How many seasons did Alan Brazil spend at Tottenham Hotspur before his transfer to Manchester United in June 1984?

177. From what London club did Town sign striker, Terry Austin, in 1974?

178. Against what "City" did Frans Thijssen play his last game for Town?

179. To the nearest 2,500, what is the club's record home attendance?

180. Can you name the "Slovan" against which Town lost 4-2 in a Penalty Shoot-Out during the 2002-2003 UEFA Cup?

PLAYERS - 2

181. Name the player who played for Town from 1973 to 1977 and for Norwich City from 1981 to 1984.

182. Name either of the 2 "Boltons" that played for Ipswich during the 1960s.

183. From what "United" did Town sign Rod Belfitt in 1971?

184. Name either the "City" from which Paul Cooper joined Town or the "City" he joined after he left Town.

185. Up to the end of the 2004-2005 season, who is the only player with a surname beginning with the letter "Z" to have played for Town?

186. What defender, in May 2000, scored Town's second goal in the Play-Off Final against Barnsley at Wembley?

187. What North East club did Phil Whelan sign for when he left Town?

188. Name the former Town striker who in August 2003 was appointed the Assistant Manager of Harvard University in Boston, USA.

189. Can you name the Town player who was named in the Scotland Squad for 2 Internationals - "Futures" Squad to play Turkey at the end of 2003 and Wales in February 2004 - but had to withdraw through injury on both occasions?

190. Who in season 1972-1973 was the first winner of the Ipswich Town Player of the Year Award?

SEASON 2004-2005 - 1

191.   What FA Premier League "United" did Town beat 2-1 in a pre-season friendly at Portman Road on 28th July 2004 in a Testimonial for Dale Roberts?

192.   Can you name the "Rovers" that put Town out of the Carling Cup in the 2nd Round?

193.   What defender scored Town's first League goal of the season?

194.   Can you recall the "County" that inflicted Town's first League defeat of the season on them?

195.   Name the Town player who scored in 3 consecutive games against Derby County, Cardiff City and Brentford.

196.   What team that would later be promoted to the FA Premier League did Town beat 2-1 at Portman Road on 21 December 2004?

197.   Can you name the London side that beat Town 2-0 at Portman Road on 26 February 2005?

198.   What "City" did Town beat 1-0 at Portman Road in their final League game of 2004?

199.   Can you name the Lancashire FA Premier League side that beat Town 3-1 at Portman Road in the FA Cup 3rd Round?

200.   Name the London team that beat Town 2-0 at Portman Road on New Year's Day.

PABLO COUNAGO

201.   What nationality is Pablo?

202.   In what year did Pablo arrive at Portman Road?

203.   Can you name the club Pablo left to join Town?

204.   To the nearest £250,000, how much did he cost Town?

205.   Against what North East club did he make his debut for Town?

206.   Can you name the Spanish side he played for from August 1998 to December 1998?

207.   What club side did Pablo play for during the 1999-2000 season?

208.   How many goals did Pablo score for Town in season 2002-2003 - 18, 19 or 20?

209.   Up to the end of the 2004-2005 season, what club has Pablo signed for twice?

210.   Can you recall the "City" against which Pablo scored his first League goal for Town?

TERRY BUTCHER

211. In what year did Terry make his Professional debut for Ipswich Town - 1976, 1977 or 1978?

212. What club did Terry sign for when he left Town?

213. To the nearest 50, how many League appearances did he make for Town?

214. In what Asian country was Terry born?

215. How many full International caps did he win - 67, 77 or 87?

216. Can you recall the "City" he joined as Player/Manager in 1990 in a £500,000 transfer?

217. Against what Scandinavian country was he playing a World Cup Qualifying game for England when he sustained a nasty head wound that by the end of the game had practically turned his white shirt red?

218. In what year did Terry captain England at the World Cup Finals?

219. Name the North East club he signed for in July 1992.

220. What Scottish club was Terry appointed the Manager of in April 2002?

LEADING GOALSCORERS
BY SEASON - 1

*ALL YOU HAVE TO DO HERE IS ASSOCIATE THE PLAYER WITH
THE SEASON HE WAS TOWN'S LEADING GOALSCORER*

221.	1968-1969	David Lowe	18
222.	1972-1973	Eric Gates	16
223.	1974-1975	Paul Mariner	17
224.	1978-1979	Marcus Bent	10
225.	1981-1982	Paul Mason	14
226.	1984-1985	Trevor Whymark	16
227.	1987-1988	John O'Rourke	17
228.	1988-1989	Bryan Hamilton	17
229.	1996-1997	Alan Brazil	28
230.	2001-2002	Dalian Atkinson	13

CUP COMPETITIONS - 1

231. In what "oil industry" sponsored Cup competition do Town have a 100% record against Norwich City?

232. Up to the end of the 2004-2005 season, how many times has Town played Norwich City in an FA Cup tie - 3, 4 or 5?

233. Can you name the "Cup" competition in which Town and Norwich City have 1 win each in Derby encounters?

234. Can you name the 1974 German World Cup winning striker who played for FC Cologne against Town in the 1980-1981 UEFA Cup?

235. Apart from John Wark, who else scored for Town against AZ 67 Alkmaar in both Legs of the 1980-1981 UEFA Cup Final?

236. Name the defender who was Town's only scorer against Barcelona in their 3-1 Penalty Shoot-Out defeat to the Spanish giants in the UEFA Cup in 1977.

237. What "Town" did Ipswich beat 2-1 in a Penalty Shoot-Out in a 1991 ZDS Cup match?

238. Who was in goal for Town when they lost to Liverpool in a Penalty Shoot-Out in their 2002 Worthington Cup tie?

239. Can you recall the "County" that put Town out of the 2003-2004 Carling Cup in Round 2?

240. What was the link between the team Town beat in the 1978 FA Cup Final and their Semi-Final game?

IPSWICH TOWN v.
MANCHESTER UNITED - 1

241.   In what year did the sides first meet - 1958, 1959 or 1960?

242.   Can you name the competition the game in Q241 was played in?

243.   This Town legend scored the winning goal in a 1-0 win over
        United in the 4th Round of the 1973-1974 FA Cup. Name the
        England International.

244.   Up to the end of the 2004-2005 season, in what year did Town
        last record a victory over United in any competition?

245.   Up to the end of the 2004-2005 season, who was the last Town
        player to score a goal for the club against United in the FA
        Premier League?

246.   What Town Manager was in charge of the club for the highest
        number of Town v. United games?

247.   This Town Manager's only game in charge of the club against
        United was a 3rd Round FA Cup 2-1 defeat on 10 January
        1988. Name him.

248.   Who was the first Town player to score a goal against United in
        the FA Premier League?

249.   Name the Town striker who, with 8 goals, has scored the most
        goals for Town against United.

250.   Can you name the legendary England centre forward who was in
        charge of Ipswich when United beat them 7-2 at Portman Road
        in a First Division game on 3 September 1963?

SEASON 2002-2003 - 1

251. In what position did Ipswich finish in the Nationwide First Division - 6th, 7th or 8th?

252. Against what "City" did Ipswich record their first home League win of the season, a 6-1 victory on 18 August?

253. Name any player that scored twice in the game in Q252.

254. Can you recall the yellow shirted team that Town beat 2-0 on 17 November?

255. What North East FA Premier League side did Town beat in Round 3 of the League Cup?

256. Name any 1 of Ipswich's last 3 League scorers during the 2002-2003 season.

257. What team won the 2002-2003 Nationwide First Division?

258. To the nearest 5, how many points did Ipswich end the season with?

259. Who was Town's leading goalscorer during the season?

260. Name the team, which would finish Runners-Up in the Nationwide First Division, that Ipswich beat at home and then also beat 2-1 away on Boxing Day.

TRIVIA - 3

261. What was Alf Ramsey's middle name - Edward, Eric or Ernest?

262. What was the score when Town played Bristol Rovers away in the 5th Round of the 1977-1978 FA Cup competition?

263. For what 'flower' Fund did Town help to raise money when they visited Cambridge City during their successful 1961-1962 Championship winning season?

264. What "Cup" competition did Norwich City put Town out of in 1980-1981?

265. Up to the end of the 2004-2005 season, what is the highest number of consecutive games played by Town without recording a win - 13, 23 or 33?

266. What "City" did Town beat 3-2 away in the FA Cup 3rd Round on 2 January 1982 and 3-2 at home in the First Division on 5 January 1982?

267. What was Ipswich elected to on 30 May 1938?

268. Name the Town Manager who signed Tommy Miller for the club in the summer of 2001.

269. Against what country, the hosts of a World Cup Final, did Mick Mills play in his last International for England?

270. What North East club put Ipswich out of the FA Cup during the 2003-2004 season?

PLAYERS - 3

271.   Can you name the first England player to be sent off in an International and who played alongside Mick Mills at Portsmouth?

272.   What "Jimmy" was the first Town player to score against Manchester United in a League Cup tie?

273.   Name any 1 of Town's 3 goalscorers in their 3-1 win over WBA in the 1978 FA Cup Semi-Final.

274.   Can you name the former Town player who played for the club from 1971 to 1975 and who in June 1998 was appointed Director of Football at Norwich City?

275.   How many times was Russell Osman sent off while playing for Ipswich - 1, 2 or 3?

276.   Can you name the 2004-2005 Town player who had loan spells at Barnsley and Millwall?

277.   Name the Town striker who scored twice away to St Etienne in the 1980-1981 UEFA Cup.

278.   Who is the only player to have been voted the Ipswich Town Player of the Year on 4 occasions by the fans?

279.   Name the defender who is the only outfield player to have played in 2 competitive Penalty Shoot-Outs for Town and missed from the spot on both occasions.

280.   Who scored a hat-trick for Town in their 4-1 home win over Watford during the 2003-2004 season?

BRYAN HAMILTON

281. In what year did Bryan sign for Town - 1970, 1971 or 1972?

282. From what Irish League side did Ipswich purchase Bryan?

283. Can you name the Lancashire side against which Bryan made his debut for Town?

284. To the nearest 10, how many appearances did Bryan make during his Town career?

285. What Merseyside club did Bryan join when he left Portman Road?

286. What team did Bryan manage between 1994 and 1998?

287. How many appearances did he make for Northern Ireland - 49, 50 or 51?

288. Can you recall the London club he joined when he left the team in Q285?

289. What other "Town" in the Football League did Bryan play for during his career?

290. Name the "Rovers" he signed for in October 1980.

THE 1970s - 1

291. Name the "Bill" who played his last game for Town (his 459th appearance) during the 1970-1971 season.

292. Name any Cup won by Town during the 1972-1973 season.

293. In what position did Town finish in the First Division at the end of the 1976-1977 season?

294. What club put Town out of Europe for the second successive year in a row during season 1978-1979?

295. Name any season during the 1970s in which Town finished in 3rd place in the First Division.

296. What national newspaper-sponsored Tournament did Town win in the 1977-1978 season?

297. Can you name the beaten Finalists in the 1976 FA Cup Final who claimed the 4th UEFA Cup place for English teams ahead of Town for season 1976-1977?

298. Name the English-born player who was Town's top goalscorer in season 1975-1976 with 15 goals in all competitions.

299. Can you name the London club over which Town did a League double in 1976-1977, beating them 3-1 at home and 4-1 away?

300. This non-English-born player was Ipswich Town's Player of the Year for season 1975-1976. Name him.

SEASON 1992-1993
FIRST SEASON IN THE
PREMIER LEAGUE

301. What Midlands club was the first team that Town met in the FA Premier League?

302. Can you name the "Gavin" who scored Town's first goal in the new FA Premier League?

303. Name the London club that was the first team Town beat in the Premier League.

304. In what position did Town finish in the League at the end of the season - 15th, 16th or 17th?

305. Who was Town's leading goalscorer, with 17 goals, during the 1992-1993 season?

306. Name the Town Manager in season 1992-1993.

307. What "Athletic" did Town beat in the League Cup 2nd Round over 2 Legs?

308. This London club beat Town 4-2 at Portman Road in the FA Cup 6th Round. Name them.

309. How many League wins did Town record during the season - 10, 11 or 12?

310. Can you name the "Frank" who was given a Testimonial game against West Ham United prior to the start of the season?

BOBBY FERGUSON

311.   In what year was Bobby appointed the Ipswich Town Manager?

312.   Who did Bobby succeed as Manager?

313.   What seaside club did Town play in his first game in charge of the team?

314.   Can you recall the year Bobby first joined Town - 1971, 1972 or 1973?

315.   Following on from Q314, what position at the club did he hold first when he arrived at Portman Road?

316.   In what position in Division One did Town finish at the end of Bobby's first season in charge of the club - 8th, 9th or 10th?

317.   At the end of what season were Town relegated under his management?

318.   To the nearest 50, for how many games was he in charge of Town?

319.   In what year did he resign and leave Portman Road?

320.   Can you recall the London club Town played in his last game in charge?

TOWN IN EUROPE - 1

321. In what season did Town participate in the European Cup?

322. What player has played the most games for Town in European competitions?

323. To the nearest 10, how many European ties has Town played in up to the end of the 2004-2005 season?

324. In which of the 3 major European competitions has Town played the most games?

325. How many of their European home games have Town lost?

326. What Spanish club were the visitors to Portman Road when their record home European attendance was set?

327. Who holds the record for having scored the most European goals for Town?

328. Apart from Mick Mills, who has captained Town in 10 or more European games?

329. To the nearest 5, how many different Town players have scored for the club in European competitions (up to the end of the 2004-2005 season)?

330. How far did Town progress in the 1978-1979 European Cup Winners' Cup?

THE UEFA CUP

331. This Brazilian World Cup star from the 1982 Finals in Spain played for AS Roma against Town in the 1982-1983 UEFA Cup. Name him.

332. What "railway sounding" Eastern European side put Town out of the UEFA Cup in 1973-1974?

333. What Dutch side did Town beat in the UEFA Cup in 1973-1974 but lost to in the 1974-1975 UEFA Cup?

334. Can you name the Scottish club which put Town, the holders, out of the UEFA Cup in 1981-1982?

335. Following on from Q334, can you name the player from the opposition who went on to manage 2 teams in the FA Premier League?

336. Name the Belgian club that put Town out of the UEFA Cup in 1975-1976.

337. Can you recall the Russian side that Town beat in the 1st Round of the 2001-2002 UEFA Cup?

338. Town lost to this Swiss side in the 2nd Round of the 1979-1980 UEFA Cup. Name them.

339. Name the Serie A side that put Town out of the UEFA Cup in 2001-2002.

340. Following on from Q339, what Brazilian superstar was a substitute in Town's away tie for the Serie A team?

FULL MEMBERS CUP - 1

341. In what year during the 1980s was the Full Members Cup introduced?

342. What happened in the year in Q341 that brought about the introduction of the Full Members Cup?

343. Can you recall the season in which Town first took part in the competition?

344. What predominantly "Green" team were Town's first opponents in the Full Members Cup?

345. How far did Town go in their first Full Members Cup tournament?

346. Name the Manager who was in charge of Town for 3 Full Members Cup competitions.

347. Can you name the London club who were Town's last opponents in the Full Members Cup?

348. This "David" scored a hat-trick for Town in their 4-1 home win over Watford on 21 November 1989. Name him.

349. In how many Full Members Cup competitions did Town participate - 5, 6 or 7?

350. Can you recall the name of the company, comprising 3 letters, that were the Sponsors of the Full Members Cup in the last season it was played for?

TRIVIA - 4

351. Against what Yorkshire "United" have there been more players sent off in games involving Town than against any other club?

352. What "Avenue" did Town beat in the FA Cup in December 1953 after a Replay?

353. To the nearest 25, how many League games did Town win under Bobby Ferguson's management?

354. In what position did Town finish in the First Division in Joe Royle's first full season in charge of the club?

355. How many times did the club win Division 3 South?

356. What "City" did Town beat 3-1 away on Christmas Day 1953 and 4-1 at home on Boxing Day 1953?

357. In March 1962 Town played and beat, at Portman Road, 2 clubs from the same City in First Division games in the space of one week. Name either team.

358. What team with an "X" in their name did Town beat in the League Cup during season 1997-1998?

359. What forced Town's game against Coventry City in 1972 to be abandoned?

360. In what year did John Lyall step down as the Manager of Ipswich Town?

PLAYERS - 4

361. What Town player became the first English-born player to score 5 goals in a single European game in Town's 10-0 home win over Floriana in 1962?

362. To the nearest £100,000 how much did Town receive from Arsenal for Brian Talbot?

363. What seaside club did Dave Linighan join when he left Town in 1996?

364. This striker played in 15 Ipswich v. Norwich Derby games for Town from 1977 to 1985, scoring twice. Name him.

365. Can you name the former Town striker who signed for Fenerbahce in August 1995?

366. This former Town striker played for Port Vale from January 1999 to October 1999 before leaving Ipswich in 2004. Name him.

367. This former striker played for 3 other "Towns" after he left Ipswich - Mansfield, Huddersfield and Northampton. Who is he?

368. What "David" was Town's leading goal scorer during the 1989-1990 season with 13 goals?

369. Who was Town's leading goalscorer in the FA Cup, with 8 goals, during their successful 1961-1962 Championship winning season?

370. What is the name of the horse-racing club run by former Town player Alan Brazil?

IPSWICH IN THE FA CUP - 1

371.   What Lancashire team put Ipswich, the holders, out of the FA Cup in season 1978-1979?

372.   What Northern "United" were the first team Ipswich had to play in defence of winning the Cup in 1978?

373.   Name the London club, and former Cup winners, that Town beat 3-0 in the 4th Round in season 1993-1994.

374.   Can you recall the Welsh club that Town beat in the Cup during season 1983-1984?

375.   This team put Town out of the FA Cup in both 1975-1976 and 1976-1977 in a 4th Round Replay. Name them.

376.   What "Mick" scored in Town's 2-1 FA Cup 3rd Round Replay win over Newcastle United in 1970-1971?

377.   These former South Coast winners of the FA Cup put Town out of the 1999-2000 competition. Name them.

378.   What seaside team did Town beat 4-0 in the 3rd Round of the FA Cup in 2002-2003?

379.   Can you recall the "City", a Premier League side in 2004-2005, that put Town out of the FA Cup in a 5th Round Replay in 1966-1967?

380.   Town put the reigning FA Premier League Champions out of the 1995-1996 FA Cup in a 1-0 3rd Round Replay away win. Name the team.

BLUES' PLAYER OF THE YEAR - 2

*ALL YOU HAVE TO DO HERE IS ASSOCIATE THE PLAYER
WITH THE SEASON HE WAS VOTED THE IPSWICH TOWN
PLAYER OF THE YEAR BY THE FANS*

381.	2002-2003	John Wark
382.	2000-2001	Trevor Putney
383.	1996-1997	Kevin Beattie
384.	1991-1992	Matt Holland
385.	1986-1987	Terry Butcher
386.	1984-1985	George Burley
387.	1983-1984	Romeo Zondervan
388.	1980-1981	Marcus Stewart
389.	1976-1977	Paul Cooper
390.	1973-1974	Mauricio Taricco

JOHN WARK - 1

391. Where in Scotland was John born - Aberdeen, Glasgow or Edinburgh?

392. Against what "United" did John make his first Town debut?

393. In what year did John make his debut for Town in his first spell at Portman Road?

394. To the nearest 50, how many League appearances did John make for Town during his playing career?

395. Can you recall the year in which John left Portman Road for the first time?

396. Following on from Q395, what club did he sign for?

397. How many full International caps did he win for Scotland - 29, 39 or 49?

398. How much did Town pay to re-sign John from the team in Q396 - £100,000, £125,000 or £150,000?

399. Can you recall the name of the club he signed for in August 1990?

400. How many different times did John sign for Ipswich as a player?

COMINGS AND GOINGS - 2

*ALL YOU HAVE TO DO HERE IS ASSOCIATE THE PLAYER
WITH THE TEAM HE LEFT TO JOIN IPSWICH OR THE
TEAM HE JOINED AFTER LEAVING IPSWICH*

401.	Darren Ambrose	to Leicester City
402.	Jason Cundy	from Millwall
403.	David Johnson	from Portsmouth
404.	Kevin O'Callaghan	to Manchester United
405.	David Geddis	from Glasgow Celtic
406.	Tony Mowbray	from Tottenham Hotspur
407.	Arnold Muhren	to Aston Villa
408.	Mick Mills	to Newcastle United
409.	Russell Osman	from Plymouth Argyle
410.	Paul Mariner	to Liverpool

PORTMAN ROAD

411.   In 1892 what Lancashire club became the first Professional side to visit Portman Road for a match with the Suffolk County FA?

412.   What was Portman Road used as from 1914 to 1918?

413.   Can you recall what became a regular feature at Portman Road in 1960 to assist viewing and remains a regular feature today?

414.   This players' safety feature was installed at the ground in 1995. Name it.

415.   What did Portman Road become the first one of in England in 1992?

416.   Name the famous American Evangelist who hired the ground as part of his "Mission England" crusade in 1984.

417.   Can you recall what was installed under Portman Road in 1972?

418.   In 1926 what had to be chased from the Grandstand before the game could be played?

419.   What type of "racing" first took place at Portman Road in 1922?

420.   This TV programme's cameras visited Portman Road for the first time in 1968. Name the TV programme.

CUP COMPETITIONS - 2

421. How many seasons did Town play in the Anglo-Italian Cup - 1, 2 or 3?

422. What type of local "Hire" company sponsored the Willhire Cup that Town played in from 1978 to 1980?

423. What team did Town meet in the FA Cup in 3 consecutive seasons during the early 1970s?

424. How many games has Town played in the European Cup?

425. What London club did Town beat in the 1989-1990 and 1990-1991 Full Members Cup competition?

426. Who scored Town's last goal during their successful 1980-1981 UEFA Cup campaign?

427. Name any 1 of Town's 3 goalscorers in their 2003-2004 FA Cup campaign.

428. Can you name the Town player who is the only Ipswich player to have reached the World Cup Semi-Finals whilst a player with the club?

429. Can you name the first Town player to be booked at the World Cup Finals?

430. Name the Scottish "holy sounding" team that Town met in the Texaco Cup in season 1972-1973.

SEASON 1980-1981
SO NEAR, YET SO FAR

431.   Name the Dutch team that Town lost 2-0 away to in a pre-season friendly.

432.   Can you recall the "City" that Town beat 1-0 away on the opening day of the season?

433.   Who scored Town's goal in Q432?

434.   Against what "3-worded team" did Town record their first League loss of the season?

435.   Name the Town striker who was the club's second highest League goalscorer during the 1980-1981 season with 17 goals.

436.   Who was Town's highest leading goalscorer in Cup competitions for the season with 18 goals?

437.   Town ended the season in Runners-Up position in the First Division. Who were crowned Champions?

438.   What South Coast club beat Town 3-2 at Portman Road in the last game of the season?

439.   To the nearest 10, how many League points did Town have at the end of the season?

440.   By how many points did the team in Q437 win the Championship over Town?

FINAL LEAGUE POSITIONS - 2

ALL YOU HAVE TO DO HERE IS ASSOCIATE TOWN WITH THEIR FINAL POSITION IN THE LEAGUE FOR THE SEASON MENTIONED (FOR EXAMPLE 1962-1963 Div 1 - ?)

441.	1962-1963	Div 1	12th
442.	1965-1966	Div 2	2nd
443.	1969-1970	Div 1	3rd
444.	1972-1973	Div 1	18th
445.	1976-1977	Div 1	20th
446.	1980-1981	Div 1	17th
447.	1983-1984	Div 1	1st
448.	1985-1986	Div 1	3rd
449.	1991-1992	Div 2	4th
450.	1998-1999	Div 1	15th

TRIVIA - 5

451. Name either of the 2 "United's" that Town met in the Willhire Cup.

452. In what position in Division 1 did Town finish at the end of the 1977-1978 season - 16th, 17th or 18th?

453. In what year did Shefki Kuqi make his International debut for Finland?

454. Where in Northern Ireland was Bryan Hamilton born - Belfast, Derry or Lisburn?

455. Name the "Sammy" who was Assistant Manager at Town during Bill McGarry's reign as Manager and who played 48 times for Norwich City, scoring 9 times, from 1955 to 1957.

456. Up to the end of the 2004-2005 season, what is the highest number of consecutive defeats suffered by Ipswich - 10, 15 or 20?

457. When Ipswich was elected to the Football League in 1938, in what Division had they been playing?

458. Can you name the Major Finals that Alf Ramsey failed to ensure England qualified for?

459. Can you name the British actor who is a Town fan and who starred in *Chariots of Fire* (1981), *A Passage to India* (1984) and *Empire of the Sun* (1987)?

460. At what ground did Town lose their 1981 FA Cup Semi-Final tie?

PLAYERS - 5

461. Name the "Ian" that scored for Town in the 1989-1990 and
1990-1991 Full Members Cup competitions.

462. Who scored 4 goals for Town in their 5-1 UEFA Cup 1st Round,
1st Leg win over Aris Salonika during their successful
1980-1981 UEFA Cup campaign?

463. Name the only Town player to score a hat-trick during their
successful 1977-1978 FA Cup winning run.

464. Can you name the Northern Ireland International who scored in
both League games against Manchester United during the
1972-1973 season?

465. Can you name the 2004-2005 Town player who tasted Play-Off
defeat with Hartlepool United on 2 occasions?

466. Name either of the 2 Ipswich players from the 1970s and 1980s
who were members of TheFA.com's Selection Panel during the
2004-2005 season.

467. This future Town Manager played for Ipswich during their
successful 1980-1981 UEFA Cup campaign. Name him.

468. Who scored both goals for Town in their 2-1 League away win
over West Ham United on Boxing Day 2003?

469. Who is the only Town player to have taken a spot kick in a World
Cup Penalty Shoot-Out and scored?

470. This "Adam" scored Town's first ever goal in the Anglo Italian
Cup. Name him.

FA CUP GLORY

471.   Who did Town beat in the 1978 FA Cup Final?

472.   Can you name the scorer of the winning goal in the Final?

473.   Who captained Ipswich to FA Cup glory in 1978?

474.   What Welsh "City" did Town beat 2-0 away in the 3rd Round of the Cup?

475.   Following on from Q474, can you recall the striker who scored both goals for Town?

476.   What lower League "United" did Town beat 4-1 at Portman Road in Round 4 of the Cup?

477.   Apart from the player in Q475, can you name any other Town goalscorer from the game in Q476?

478.   What "Rovers" did Town beat 3-0 in a 5th Round Replay at Portman Road?

479.   Can you name the Midlands club Town beat in the Semi-Final?

480.   Following on from Q479, at what London Stadium did Town play their FA Cup Semi-Final tie?

THE LEAGUE CUP - 1

481.   Who scored a hat-trick for Town in the 1983-1984 League Cup competition?

482.   Who was the only Town player to score for the team in the 1982-1983 competition?

483.   Can you name the lower Division team, whose name starts and ends with the same letter (e.g., Shamrock Rovers), that Town beat 5-0 in the 1977-1978 League Cup?

484.   What Yorkshire club was the first side that Town met in the League Cup?

485.   Name the team with three "L's" in their name that beat Town in the 1963-1964 competition.

486.   These "Rovers" put Town out of the Cup in 2004-2005. Name them.

487.   Can you name either of Town's 2 goalscorers in the 2004-2005 competition?

488.   Who was the Town Manager when they beat Brighton & Hove Albion in the 1st Round of the Cup in 2002-2003?

489.   How many goals did Town score in the League Cup in the two seasons, 1978-1979 and 1979-1980?

490.   Town beat two Yorkshire teams in the League Cup in season 1981-1982. Name either of the 2.

LEADING GOALSCORERS
BY SEASON - 2

*ALL YOU HAVE TO DO HERE IS ASSOCIATE THE PLAYER
WITH THE SEASON HE WAS TOWN'S LEADING GOALSCORER*

491.	1967-1968	Trevor Whymark	15
492.	1971-1972	Pablo Counago	20
493.	1975-1976	Kevin Wilson	25
494.	1979-1980	Claus Thomsen	5
495.	1982-1983	Paul Mariner	22
496.	1986-1987	Chris Kiwomya	12
497.	1990-1991	John Wark	23
498.	1994-1995	Mick Hill	8
499.	1999-2000	Ray Crawford	21
500.	2002-2003	David Johnson	23

ARNOLD MUHREN

501.   In what year did Arnold sign for Town - 1977, 1978 or 1979?

502.   What BBC TV Match of the Day commentator once described Arnold as "The Man with Velvet Feet"?

503.   Can you name the Lancashire side against which Arnold made his debut for Town?

504.   To the nearest 10, how many appearances did Arnold make during his Town career?

505.   From what Dutch club, whose name sounds like a number, did Arnold join Town?

506.   What team did Arnold join when he left Portman Road?

507.   In what year did he leave Portman Road to join the team in Q506?

508.   Can you recall the medal he won in 1983?

509.   With what Dutch club did Arnold begin his Professional career?

510.   To the nearest 5, how many International caps did he win for Holland during his time at Portman Road?

TREVOR WHYMARK

511. In what year did Trevor arrive at Portman Road - 1968, 1969 or 1970?

512. Can you name any 1 of the 3 "United's" that Trevor played for between 1984 and 1985?

513. Against what First Division "City", and reigning League Champions, did he make his debut for Town?

514. Can you name the Canadian North American Soccer League side he left in December 1980?

515. What "County" did Trevor sign for in December 1979?

516. To the nearest 25, how many goals did Trevor score for Town during his time at Portman Road?

517. In what year did he retire from playing Professional football - 1985, 1986 or 1987?

518. How many full International caps did he win with England - 1, 2 or 3?

519. Trevor won 7 England Under-23 caps. How many goals did he score in these 7 games - 2, 4 or 7?

520. To the nearest 10, how many appearances did he make for Town?

SEASON 2000-2001

521. Name the Dutch or the Italian team that Town played in a pre-season Friendly at Portman Road.

522. Can you recall the London side that Town lost 3-1 away to on the opening day of the season?

523. What "Mark" scored Town's first Premier League goal of the season?

524. Against what "United" did Town record their first away League win of the season?

525. Name the Town player who scored in 7 consecutive games from 26 December to 20 January.

526. What 'Alan' was Town's second highest leading goalscorer for the season with 8 goals?

527. In what position in the Premier League did Town finish at the end of the season - 5th, 6th or 7th?

528. What "City" did Town beat 2-1 in their last home game of season?

529. To the nearest 10, how many League points did Town have at the end of the season?

530. Name the Midlands team that beat Town 2-1 at Portman Road and 2-1 at their own ground.

Photographs © www.sporting-heroes.net

THE MANAGERS

ALL YOU HAVE TO DO IS ASSOCIATE THE MANAGER WITH THE PERIOD HE WAS IN CHARGE AT PORTMAN ROAD (APPROXIMATE DATES)

	MANAGER	FROM	TO
531.	George Burley	12.11.1937	07.08.1955
532.	Bobby Robson	05.10.1964	23.11.1968
533.	Jackie Milburn	19.08.1982	17.05.1987
534.	John Lyall	08.08.1955	30.04.1963
535.	Bobby Ferguson	13.01.1969	18.08.1982
536.	A Scott Duncan	01.05.1963	08.09.1964
537.	Bill McGarry	28.12.1994	11.10.2002
538.	John Duncan	09.09.1964	04.10.1964
539.	Alf Ramsey	17.06.1987	05.05.1990
540.	Jimmy Forsyth (Caretaker)	11.05.1990	05.12.1994

TRIVIA - 6

541. Can you recall the "first" that Arnold Muhren achieved at Wembley in 1983?

542. To the nearest 2,500, what was Town's average home League attendance during their successful 1961-1962 Championship winning season?

543. What team beat Town over 2 Legs in the Championship Play-Offs in May 2005?

544. What 'Alex' was Town's leading goalscorer during the 1995-1996 season with 19 goals?

545. In what position in Division 1 did Town finish at the end of the 1975-1976 season - 6th, 7th or 8th?

546. What team beginning with the letter 'P' is the only English side that Town played in the Anglo-Italian Cup?

547. Despite winning the Texaco Cup in 1973, beating Norwich in the Final, why were Town unable to defend the trophy the following season?

548. What club was Bryan Hamilton appointed the Manager of on 5 April 2000?

549. What team did Shefki Kuqi join in June 2005?

550. Name the relegated London club that Town beat home and away in the League during the 2003-2004 season.

PLAYERS - 6

551. Can you name the first Town player to play in the World Cup Finals (Final Stages)?

552. What "Ray" is Town's second highest all-time leading goalscorer in the League Cup with 10 goals?

553. Who was Town's leading goalscorer during the 1970-1971 season with 12 goals?

554. What "Paul" scored 3 goals for Town in their only ever participation in the Anglo-Italian Cup during the 1995-1996 season?

555. Name the "Clive" who scored in both League games against Manchester United during the 1976-1977 season?

556. Can you name the "Alec" who was a former Town trainee and played in goal for Luton Town when Ipswich beat them 2-1 in a Penalty Shoot-Out in a 1991 ZDS Cup match?

557. How many games did Terry Butcher play for England at the World Cup Finals - 9, 10 or 11?

558. From what "City" did Gerry Creaney join Ipswich on loan during the 1996-1997 season?

559. Name the midfielder who joined Ipswich in 2001, 5 years after he was told he was not required by the club when he was just 15?

560. In the 1988 European Championships Final, Arnold Muhren laid on an inch-perfect pass to a teammate who scored a goal from a remarkable angle. Name the scorer of the "wonder strike".

HIGHEST AGGREGATE
SCORE IN HOME GAMES

ALL YOU HAVE TO DO HERE IS ASSOCIATE THE
SCORE WITH THE OPPOSITION

561.	Won 11-0	Leyton Orient (Division 2)	02.01.1960
562.	Won 8-2	Lowestoft Town (FA Cup)	21.10.1936
563.	Won 10-0	Aldershot (Division 3 South)	26.04.1939
564.	Won 6-4	Stowmarket (FA Cup)	03.10.1936
565.	Won 7-2	Avenir Beggen (UEFA Cup)	29.08.2002
566.	Won 6-3	Floriana (European Cup)	25.09.1962
567.	Lost 2-7	Cromer (FA Cup)	31.10.1936
568.	Won 8-1	Manchester United (Division 1)	03.09.1963
569.	Won 8-0	Crewe Alexandra (Division 1)	17.01.2004
570.	Won 7-1	Newport County Reserves (Southern League)	16.10.1937

SCORING DEBUTANTS - 1

ALL YOU HAVE TO DO HERE IS ASSOCIATE THE PLAYER WITH THE TEAM HE SCORED AGAINST ON HIS TOWN DEBUT

571.	David Unsworth	Coventry City
572.	Darren Currie	Cardiff City
573.	Shefki Kuqi	Swansea City
574.	Martijn Reuser	Oldham Athletic
575.	Marcus Stewart	Sheffield United
576.	Jason Dozzell	Barnsley
577.	Colin Viljoen	Watford
578.	Ian Marshall	Fulham
579.	John O'Rourke	Portsmouth
580.	Ray Crawford	Queens Park Rangers

I LEFT TOWN AND JOINED CITY

ALL YOU HAVE TO DO HERE IS ASSOCIATE THE PLAYER WITH THE "CITY" HE LEFT TOWN FOR

581.	Geoff Hammond	Cardiff City
582.	Ken Thompson	Bradford City
583.	Keith Bertschin	Manchester City
584.	Richie Appleby	Coventry City
585.	Gary Croft	Hull City
586.	Louie Donowa	Norwich City
587.	John Miller	Birmingham City
588.	John O'Rourke	Bristol City
589.	Neil Woods	Exeter City
590.	Bill Baxter	Swansea City

SHEFKI KUQI

591.   In what year did Shefki join Town?

592.   From what Yorkshire club did Town sign Shefki?

593.   What "County" did Shefki play for prior to joining the team in Q592?

594.   To the nearest £150,000, how much did the team in Q592 pay for his services?

595.   Name either of the 2 'Helsinki' clubs that Shefki played for.

596.   In what Eastern European country was Shefki born?

597.   How many games did Shefki play for Town on loan prior to signing for the club - 9, 10 or 11?

598.   Following on from Q597, how many goals did he score in these games?

599.   To the nearest £50,000, how much did the "County" in Q593 pay for him?

600.   Can you name the German club that was interested in signing Shefki prior to the start of the 2004-2005 season, only for him to turn them down?

SQUAD NUMBERS 2004-2005 - 2

ALL YOU HAVE TO DO HERE IS ASSOCIATE THE PLAYER WITH HIS SQUAD NUMBER FOR THE 2004-2005 SEASON

601.	Adem Atay	No. 8
602.	Drissa Diallo	No. 22
603.	Shane Supple	No. 20
604.	Dean McDonald	No. 28
605.	Aidan Collins	No. 5
606.	Tommy Miller	No. 3
607.	Matthew Richards	No. 27
608.	Gerard Nash	No. 7
609.	Jim Magilton	No. 31
610.	Darryl Knights	No. 15

BLUES SEEING RED

611.   What Town player was sent off in a home game against Plymouth Argyle on 25 September 2004?

612.   Can you name the Derby County striker, and scorer of the winning goal in the 1971 FA Cup Final, who was sent off with Town's John Wark on 14 May 1977?

613.   When playing against what "City" was Paul Mariner sent off on 23 October 1982?

614.   Name the Town player, whose Christian name and surname both begin with the same letter, who was given his marching orders in a Division 1 away game at Norwich City on 7 March 2004.

615.   Can you name the Town player, with the same surname as a football team that the legendary Pele played for, who was dismissed during Ipswich's Division 1 game at Millwall on 13 December 2003?

616.   Name any Town player that was sent off during the 2002-2003 season.

617.   This "Steve" was sent off in Town's FA Cup 6th Round tie at Everton on 9 March 1985. Name him.

618.   What Town defender was given an early bath in a Division 1 game away to Southampton on 8 November 1980?

619.   Can you recall the "Colin" who was given his marching orders at home to Wolves on 21 April 1973?

620.   Name the UEFA Champions League winner who was sent off while playing for Spurs against Town in an FA Premier League game at White Hart Lane on 22 December 2001.

PAUL COOPER

621. In what year did Paul join Town - 1972, 1973 or 1974?

622. From what Birmingham based club did Town sign Paul?

623. What "City" did Paul join when he left Portman Road?

624. Against what "United" did he make his Town debut in a First Division game?

625. In what year did he leave Town?

626. Can you recall the London club against which Paul played his last game for Town?

627. To the nearest 100, how many games did Paul play for Town?

628. Name the "County" he joined in August 1990.

629. To the nearest 5, how many appearances did he make in his last season with Town?

630. Apart from the "City's" in Q622 and Q623, can you name another "City" that Paul played for?

PAUL MARINER

631. In what year did Paul arrive at Portman Road - 1974, 1975 or 1976?

632. Can you name the non-League side beginning with the letter 'C' that Paul played for before he joined Town?

633. Against what First Division "United" did he make his debut for Town?

634. To the nearest 5, how many full International caps did he win for England?

635. What London side did Paul sign for when he left Portman Road?

636. To the nearest 10, how many goals did Paul score for Town during his time at Portman Road?

637. In what year did he leave Ipswich to join the team in Q635?

638. Can you recall the famous Lancashire Town where Paul was born?

639. At what South Coast club did he end his Professional career?

640. Against what "City" did he make his last appearance for Town?

TRIVIA - 7

641.   What trademark "bird dive" does Shefki Kuqi perform when he scores?

642.   To the nearest 20, how many different England players did Alf Ramsey cap during his reign as England Manager?

643.   What Dutch club did Arnold Muhren re-join when he left Manchester United?

644.   Up to the end of the 2004-2005 season, how many games, to the nearest 10, have Town won in their 148 League Cup matches?

645.   Who was Town's leading goalscorer during the 1997-1998 season with 22 goals?

646.   In what position in Division 2 did Town finish at the end of the 1966-1967 season - 5th, 6th or 7th?

647.   Who is the only man to have managed Town in the Willhire Cup?

648.   Can you name any 1 of the 4 Italian sides that Town played in the Anglo-Italian Cup?

649.   Can you recall the North East First Division side that Town played during the 1997-1998 season when 3 players were sent off at Portman Road?

650.   To the nearest 5, with how many League points did Town finish the 2003-2004 season?

PLAYERS - 7

651. Name the "Charlie" who scored on his Town debut against Brentford in an away League Cup 2nd Round tie in 1966.

652. Who wore No. 26 during season 2004-2005 for Town?

653. Who, with 19 goals, was Town's leading goalscorer in the FA Premier League during season 2000-2001?

654. Name any 1 of the 5 Town players who scored a total of 8 League Cup goals for the club during his career at Portman Road.

655. What Northern Ireland International played 23 times for Town in the 1975-1976 season, scoring 5 times, and then left them for Everton?

656. How many times was Paul Mariner sent off playing for Ipswich - 2, 3 or 4?

657. With what club did Arnold Muhren win a European Cup winners' medal in 1971?

658. Can you name the "City" against which Shefki Kuqi scored a 20 yard goal to earn Town a place in the 2003-2004 Play-Offs?

659. Name any 1 of Town's 3 goalscorers in their 3-0 First Division home win over Manchester United on 10 April 1976.

660. Can you recall the club to which Amir Karic was on loan when he played for Slovenia at the 2002 World Cup Finals?

THE HISTORY - 2

661. What "Ray" holds the record for having scored the most goals for the club?

662. Can you name the Northern Ireland International who is Ipswich Town's most capped player?

663. Up to the end of the 2004-2005 season, what player holds the record for being the club's most expensive signing?

664. Against what Midlands club did Ipswich record the worst ever Cup loss, a 6-2 reversal, on 30 November 1988?

665. Can you name the London club that inflicted Town's worst ever League loss when they lost 10-1 on 26 December 1963 in a First Division game?

666. How many times has Ipswich won the FA Cup?

667. In what European competition did Ipswich record their best ever Cup win, a 10-0 home win, on 25 September 1962?

668. Following on from Q667, what Maltese side beginning with the letter "F" did they beat?

669. "Suicide is Painless" was No. 1 in the UK charts when Terry Butcher made his England debut. What show was the song the theme song to?

670. How many times did Ipswich win Football League Division 2?

DERBY DAYS: IPSWICH TOWN v. NORWICH CITY - 2

671.   Can you name the Town defender who played in 23 Derby games from 1966-1981?

672.   Who with 9 goals has scored the most goals in Derby games?

673.   Name the "Paul" who has made the 3rd most Derby appearances for Town with 22 between 1975-1985.

674.   In what "Cup" competition did City beat Town 1-0 at Carrow Road on 19 February 1983?

675.   Can you recall the "Richard" who made 6 Derby appearances for Town between 1996 and 2004?

676.   Name the striker that played in 15 Derby games between 1977 and 1983, scoring 5 times.

677.   Who played for Town from 1969 to 1980 and for City from 1980 to 1982?

678.   In what 3 domestic "Cup" competitions have the 2 sides met?

679.   In what "local" League did the 2 teams play 6 times, with Town winning 1, drawing 1 and losing 4?

680.   To the nearest 5, how many times have Town and City met in charity/friendly/testimonial games up to the end of the 2004-2005 season?

MON£Y MATT£RS

681. Can you recall the flamboyant Manager who signed Arnold Muhren from Ipswich Town in 1982?

682. To the nearest 2,500 what was Town's average League home attendance during the 2003-2004 season?

683. What was Howard Wells appointed the first one of at Ipswich Town in December 1999?

684. To the nearest £50,000, how much did Town pay for the services of Fabian Wilnis?

685. With what company did Town sign a shirt sponsorship deal in 1981?

686. To the nearest £5,000, how much did Town's first floodlight system cost when it was officially switched on in 1960?

687. From what London club did Town purchase 650 tip-up seats in 1937 to install in the Grandstand at Portman Road?

688. How much did it cost an adult to watch a game at Portman Road in 1938?

689. How much did it cost in 1911 to replace the Grandstand roof at Portman Road after it was blown off in a gale - £60, £70 or £80?

690. To the nearest £500, how much did it cost to construct the New West Stand (uncovered) terracing in 1952?

THE BOSS - JOE ROYLE

691. At what club did Joe begin his Professional career as a footballer?

692. Following on from Q691, how many years did he finish the season as the club's top goalscorer?

693. Can you recall the Lancashire side he joined in 1974?

694. What Cup did Joe win with the team in Q693 in 1976?

695. What forced Joe to hang up his boots in 1982, thus ending his playing career?

696. Can you recall the club that gave him his first taste of management experience and where he stayed for 12 years?

697. Name the club he became the Manager of after leaving the team in Q696.

698. In what year did he guide the team in Q697 to FA Cup glory when his side beat Manchester United in the Final?

699. To the nearest 5, how many full International caps did he win with England?

700. In what year was Joe appointed the Boss of Town?

COMINGS AND GOINGS - 3

*ALL YOU HAVE TO DO HERE IS ASSOCIATE THE PLAYER
WITH THE TEAM HE LEFT TO JOIN IPSWICH OR THE TEAM
HE JOINED AFTER LEAVING IPSWICH*

701. Brian Talbot   to Derry City

702. Jimmy Robertson   to Bradford City

703. Micky Stockwell   to Arsenal

704. Matteo Sereni   to Manchester City

705. Alan Sunderland   from Diss Town

706. Romeo Zondervan   to Norwich City

707. Eddie Youds   from Arsenal

708. Trevor Whymark   to Colchester United

709. Colin Viljoen   from West Bromwich Albion

710. Clive Woods   from Sampdoria

THE 1980s - 2

711.   Name any season in which Town finished Runners-Up in English League Division 1.

712.   Name Ipswich's Dutch star who was voted the Football Writers' Player of the Year in season 1980-1981.

713.   Name the player who was voted Town's Player of the Year in seasons 1984-1985 and 1985-1986.

714.   Can you recall the "United" that Kevin Beattie signed for when he left Ipswich in 1981?

715.   Over what 2 "United's" did Town record League double victories during the 1981-1982 season?

716.   Name the Ipswich defender who came second in the voting for the Football Writers' Player of the Year in season 1980-1981.

717.   What Town striker was voted the Ipswich Town Player of the Year in season 1982-1983?

718.   How many Town players represented their countries at the 1982 World Cup Finals in Spain?

719.   Who scored 36 League and Cup goals for Town in season 1980-1981?

720.   What was installed above the North Stand at Portman Road for the 1981-1982 season?

ALAN BRAZIL

721.   In what year did Alan sign as a Professional for Town - 1975, 1976 or 1977?

722.   Can you name the Lancashire side against which Alan made his debut for Town?

723.   To the nearest 50, how many appearances did Alan make during his Town career?

724.   What London club did Alan join when he left Portman Road?

725.   In what year did Alan leave Town?

726.   How many appearances did he make for Scotland - 11, 12 or 13?

727.   Can you recall the club he joined when he left the team in Q724?

728.   What "City" did Alan sign for in January 1986?

729.   What radio talk show does Alan Brazil co-present with Mike Parry?

730.   What season was Alan's most prolific at Town in terms of the total number of goals scored?

MICK MILLS - 2

731. Can you name the former Ipswich Town striker to whom Mick Mills offered the job of Birmingham City Youth Team Coach only for him to turn his former teammate down?

732. To the nearest 5, how many League goals did Mick Mills score for Town?

733. What was the first trophy Mick won with Ipswich Town?

734. In what year did Mick Mills make his full International debut for England - 1971, 1972 or 1973?

735. How many goals did Mick Mills score for England in a full International?

736. In what year did Mick lead Ipswich to FA Cup success?

737. Can you recall the year in which Mick Mills retired from International football?

738. How many England Under-23 caps did Mick Mills win - 5, 6 or 7?

739. To the nearest 5, how many times did Mick Mills captain England in a full International?

740. Against what team did Mick Mills make his 100th appearance for Southampton, his 900th career appearance?

UEFA CUP WINNERS - 2

741. Town beat a Polish side 5-0 at home in the 3rd Round, 1st Leg. Name them.

742. What Town striker captained the side when they played the team in Q741 away?

743. Name the German Bundesliga club that Ipswich beat in the Semi-Finals.

744. Following on from Q743, name the England centre forward who was playing for the German side.

745. Can you name the Dutch World Cup Runner-Up from 1974 and 1978 who played for St Etienne against Town in the Quarter-Finals?

746. Who scored Town's first goal in the 1980-1981 UEFA Cup competition?

747. Name the "Irish sounding" Czech side that beat Ipswich in their Round 2, 2nd Leg tie.

748. Can you name either of the 2 teams that Ipswich beat away in the competition?

749. Name any 2 of Town's 3 goalscorers in their 3-0 1st Leg Final win at Portman Road.

750. Name either of the 2 teams that Ipswich failed to score against in an away Leg of the competition.

TRIVIA - 8

751. Against what former European Championships co-hosts did Shefki Kuqi make his International debut for Finland?

752. Who wore No. 34 during season 2004-2005 for Town?

753. To the nearest 5, how many International caps did Arnold Muhren win for Holland during his time at Manchester United?

754. In season 2000-2001 Town finished 5th in the FA Premier League. Apart from the Champions, Manchester United, and Arsenal, can you name either of the other 2 teams that finished above Town?

755. To the nearest "10", how many League goals did Town score during the 2000-2001 FA Premier League season?

756. Up to the end of the 2004-2005 season, for what club has Marcus Bent scored the most goals - Everton, Leicester City or Town?

757. In what position in Division 1 did Town finish at the end of the 1984-1985 season - 16th, 17th or 18th?

758. Who is the only man to have managed Town in the Anglo-Italian Cup?

759. In what year was David Sheepshanks appointed the Chairman of Ipswich Town?

760. To the nearest 25, how many goals did Joe Royle score for Everton?

PLAYERS - 8

761.   Up to the end of the 2004-2005 season, who was the last Town
        player to score on his debut for the club?

762.   How many goals did Shefki Kuqi score for Town in season
        2003-2004 - 10, 12 or 14?

763.   What sports club did Ipswich Association merge with in 1888
        to become Ipswich Town Football Club?

764.   Who was Town's leading goalscorer during the 1998-1999
        season with 14 goals?

765.   How many appearances did former Town hero, Bryan Hamilton,
        make for Everton - 46, 48 or 50?

766.   Who wore No. 2 during season 2004-2005 for Town?

767.   Name the second Town player to score a goal in the World Cup
        Finals.

768.   Who took over the management of Town on a Caretaker basis
        from 11 to 28 October 2002?

769.   Who wore No. 18 during season 2004-2005 for Town?

770.   What winners' medal did Arnold Muhren collect in 1988?

SIR ALF RAMSEY - 2

771. Name the England Manager that Alf Ramsey succeeded.

772. In what year did he lead Town to the Second Division Championship?

773. Name either of the 2 seasons in which Ipswich won the highest number of games when Alf Ramsey was in charge.

774. To the nearest 5, for how many Cup games was Alf in charge of Town?

775. Can you recall the Lancashire club that Ipswich played in Alf's last game as Town Manager?

776. In what year was Sir Alf Ramsey sacked from his position as the England Football Team Manager?

777. To the nearest 50, for how many League games was Alf Ramsey Manager of Ipswich Town?

778. In what year did Sir Alf sadly die aged 79?

779. What competition did England win 9 times under Alf Ramsey's leadership?

780. Name the "Jimmy" who was offered the England Manager's job prior to Alf Ramsey being appointed.

BLUES' PLAYER OF THE YEAR - 3

ALL YOU HAVE TO DO HERE IS ASSOCIATE THE PLAYER WITH THE SEASON HE WAS VOTED THE IPSWICH TOWN PLAYER OF THE YEAR BY THE FANS

781.	2001-2002	Alan Brazil
782.	1998-1999	Paul Mariner
783.	1995-1996	John Wark
784.	1993-1994	Colin Viljoen
785.	1990-1991	Jamie Clapham
786.	1982-1983	Frans Thijssen
787.	1981-1982	Simon Milton
788.	1979-1980	Mick Mills
789.	1977-1978	Mark Venus
790.	1974-1975	David Linighan

FRANS THIJSSEN

791.   What nationality is Frans?

792.   In what year did Frans arrive at Portman Road?

793.   Can you name the club that Frans left to join Town?

794.   What player at Town urged Bobby Robson to purchase Frans?

795.   Name the player who had just left Town for Arsenal which
        prompted Bobby Robson to sign Frans as his replacement.

796.   Against what "County" did he make his debut for Town?

797.   In what year did Frans leave Portman Road?

798.   Can you recall the Canadian team that Frans played for in the
        North American Soccer League?

799.   What First Division club, and former European Champions, did
        Frans sign for after he left the team in Q798?

800.   How many goals did Frans score for Town in his first full season
        at the club - 3, 5 or 7?

SEASON 2003-2004 - 2

801. What team finished below Town in the League but were promoted to the FA Premier League?

802. How many League games did Town win during the season - 21, 22 or 23?

803. Name any 1 of the 3 "United's" that Town played in a pre-season friendly prior to the start of the 2003-2004 season.

804. What had the 6 teams that Town played in consecutive League games between 26 August 2003 and 27 September 2003 got in common?

805. What "County" did Town beat 3-0 in the FA Cup 3rd Round?

806. Who scored Town's last League goal of the 2003-2004 season?

807. Who scored Town's winner against West Ham United in the 1st Leg of their Semi-Final Play-Off games?

808. Town finished 5th in the League at the end of the season, but can you name 3 of the teams that finished above them?

809. Name any 1 of Town's 3 players who all scored 11 League goals during the season to tie for equal 2nd place behind Darren Bent in the goal-scoring charts.

810. Who scored a hat-trick for Town in their 3-1 away win over Walsall during the season?

FIRST DIVISION CHAMPIONS

811. In what season during the 1960s were Town crowned First Division Champions?

812. Who managed Town to Championship glory?

813. Can you recall the Lancashire side that were Runners-Up to Town?

814. To the nearest 10, with how many points did Town finish the season?

815. How many of their 42 League games did Town win - 23, 24 or 25?

816. Only 2 teams beat Town at Portman Road in a League game during the season. Manchester City was the first when they won 4-2 on 26 August. What London club was the second?

817. Who finished the season as Town's top goalscorer in the League?

818. Following on from Q817, how many League goals did he score - 33, 34 or 35?

819. What "City" put Town out of the FA Cup during their run to the Championship?

820. Ray Crawford and Ted Phillips scored 3 goals each in Town's 2 wins (3-2 at home and 3-1 away) over the reigning League Champions. Who did they beat?

SEASON 2004-2005 - 2

821. What university sounding "United" did Town beat 5-1 in a pre-season Friendly away from home?

822. Name either of the 2 clubs that Town lost to over 5 days in February 2005.

823. Can you name the Town player whose Christian name and surname both end with the same letter and who scored the winner against Stoke City in Town's last game of 2004?

824. What former Premiership "City" was the first team Town beat in 2005?

825. What team did James Scowcroft sign for on 1 July 2005?

826. Name the team, later to be relegated, that Town beat 6-0 at Portman Road on 12 March 2005.

827. Can you name either of the 2 players who scored for Town in consecutive League games against Derby County and Rotherham United?

828. Who scored Town's only FA Cup goal of the season?

829. Town had two consecutive 2-2 away draws over the course of 5 days in October. Name either of the 2 teams they played.

830. What Town player scored his first League goal of the season in Town's fourth League game, a 3-1 home win over Cardiff City?

ALL-TIME LEADING
GOALSCORERS - 1

ALL YOU HAVE TO DO HERE IS ASSOCIATE THE PLAYER WITH THE NUMBER OF GOALS HE SCORED FOR TOWN IN HIS CAREER

831.	Matt Holland	92
832.	Bryan Hamilton	47
833.	Alex Mathie	80
834.	John Wark	64
835.	Eric Gates	49
836.	Alan Brazil	45
837.	Tommy Parker	143
838.	Chris Kiwomya	179
839.	Kevin Wilson	96
840.	Tom Garneys	56

TRIVIA - 9

841. What Yorkshire club did Drissa Diallo sign for on a free transfer on 2 July 2005?

842. What "United" did Town beat in the 1988-1989 and 1991-1992 Full Members Cup competition?

843. Name any English Football League club side that Bryan Hamilton has coached or managed.

844. Up to the end of the 2004-2005 season, how many times have Town met rivals, Norwich City, in the League Cup?

845. Who became the first Town player to win an England cap when he played centre forward against Northern Ireland at Wembley on 22 November 1961?

846. What nickname, which is also the name of a movie starring Willem Dafoe, was given to Joe Royle's 1995 FA Cup winning Everton team?

847. Can you recall the player that Bobby Robson once famously described as being "as daft as a brush"?

848. How many full England International caps did Alf Ramsey win during his career - 32, 42 or 52?

849. What team, with the letter "X" in their name, did Town beat 6-4 at Portman Road in a League game on 17 January 2004?

850. Following on from Q849, can you name either of the 2 Town players that scored twice in the game?

PLAYERS - 9

851. Who, after John Wark and Trevor Whymark, is the third highest goalscorer for Town in European competitions?

852. Town have had 9 different captains in European ties. Can you name any 5 of them?

853. Can you name the "Frank" who scored in both League games against Manchester United during the 1970-1971 season?

854. This goalkeeper played for Norwich City from 1977 to 1984 and for Town from 1992 to 1995. Name him.

855. Who won an FA Cup winners' medal with Town in 1978 and another FA Cup winning medal the following year?

856. Can you name the Town defender that was linked to a move to Southampton and Newcastle United in 2003 before he signed a new 4-year deal at Ipswich?

857. Who was in goal for Town when they lost 2-0 away to Bohemians Prague in the 1980-1981 UEFA Cup?

858. Who scored a hat-trick of penalties for Town in a single Leg during their successful 1980-1981 UEFA Cup campaign?

859. Name the "Tony" who was sent off twice while playing for Town during the 1995-1996 season.

860. Who is the only Town player to have played at 3 World Cup Final Tournaments?

THE 1970s - 2

861. What season was Bryan Hamilton's best at Town in terms of the total number of goals scored?

862. Can you name the new Stand that was ready in time for the opening game of the 1971-1972 season?

863. During the 1972-1973 season Ipswich broke their record home attendance in 2 consecutive games. Name either of the other 2 sides involved.

864. Name the Italian or Spanish sides that Town beat on their way to the UEFA Quarter-Finals in season 1973-1974.

865. What Lancashire team did Town trail on 3 occasions only to pull a goal back each time to earn a 3-3 draw?

866. Who in his first season at Town won the Ipswich Town Player of the Year Award for season 1978-1979?

867. What London team were Town playing away in the FA Cup during season 1977-1978 when the game was held up for 18 minutes because of rioting by the home fans?

868. Name the player who was signed in season 1976-1977 for a then club record of £220,000.

869. In what position in Division 1 did Town finish at the end of the 1972-1973 season?

870. What Team beat Town 5-0 at Wembley in the FA Charity Shield in season 1978-1979?

MICK STOCKWELL

871.   In what year did Mick make his Professional debut for Ipswich Town - 1984, 1985 or 1986?

872.   What "United" did Mick sign for when he left Town?

873.   To the nearest 50, how many League appearances did he make for Town?

874.   In what year did Mick sign for the team in Q872?

875.   How many full International caps did he win?

876.   Can you recall the non-League "Swifts" he joined after leaving the team in Q872?

877.   How many goals did he score for Town in season 1996-1997 - 10, 11 or 12?

878.   Against what "City" did Mick make his debut for Town in a first Division game?

879.   Can you name the "County" against which he made his last appearance for Town?

880.   Name the Ridgeon's League 'Town' he signed for in September 2004.

TOWN IN EUROPE - 2

881. What Spanish team put town out of the European Cup Winners' Cup in 1978-1979?

882. Can you name the Dutch club that Town has played in 2 different European competitions?

883. To the nearest 10, how many different players have Town used in European ties up to the end of the 2004-2005 season?

884. What "Kevin" has made the most substitute appearances for Town in European competitions?

885. What goalkeeper has played the second highest number of games for Town in European competitions?

886. To the nearest 20, how many goals have Town scored in European ties up to the end of the 2004-2005 season?

887. Town have an unbeaten record in their 31 European ties at Portman Road. How many of the 31 did they actually win?

888. Who, after John Wark, is the second highest goalscorer for Town in European competitions?

889. How many ties have Town played in the European Cup Winners' Cup?

890. In what season did Town first compete in the UEFA Cup?

ERIC GATES

891. In what year did Eric sign Professional forms at Portman Road - 1971, 1972 or 1973?

892. Against what famous "Midlands" club did he make his debut for Town?

893. To the nearest 5, how many full International caps did he win for England?

894. What North East side did Eric sign for when he left Portman Road?

895. To the nearest 10, how many goals did Eric score for Town during his time at Portman Road?

896. In what year did he leave Ipswich to join the team in Q894?

897. Can you recall the England Manager who awarded Eric his first full International cap for England?

898. At what "United" did he end his Professional playing career?

899. Against what "United" did he make his last appearance for Town in a First Division game?

900. To the nearest 50, how many appearances did he make for Town?

FULL MEMBERS CUP - 2

901. In what season did Town last play in the Full Members Cup?

902. What happened in 1990 that had a dramatic effect on the tournament?

903. How many different men managed Town in a Full Members Cup game?

904. Who scored Town's last ever goal in the competition - Jason Dozzell, Chris Kiwomya or David Lowe?

905. These "Rovers" beat Town in the 1987 Semi-Finals. Name them.

906. Can you name any London club that Town played in the competition in 1989-1990?

907. Can you name the "Nigel" who scored Town's first ever goal in the competition in a 3-1 home win over Plymouth Argyle on 16 September 1986?

908. What London club put Town out of the Cup on 2 different occasions?

909. Name any Town scorer from their 5-2 win over Watford at Portman Road on 25 January 1988.

910. What 'City' beat Town in the 1990-1991 Southern Semi-Final?

IPSWICH IN THE FA CUP - 2

911. Name the team that beat Town in the 1981 FA Cup Semi-Final.

912. What "Paul" scored in the 4th and 5th Rounds of the Cup for Town in 1995-1996?

913. Name the defender who scored Town's winner at home to Liverpool in the 4th Round of the Cup in 1974-1975.

914. These former European Cup winners put Town out of the FA Cup in season 1988-1989. Name them.

915. Can you recall the Yorkshire "City" that Town drew 4-4 with in the 3rd Round of the FA Cup in season 1985-1986?

916. What "Tony" scored for Town when Manchester United won 2-1 at Portman Road in a 3rd Round FA Cup tie on 10 January 1988?

917. Name either of the 2 "United's" that Town met in the FA Cup in 1973-1974.

918. What South Coast club beat Town 7-1 in the 3rd Round of the FA Cup in season 1960-1961?

919. How many games did Town play in the FA Cup during the 1952-1953 season before going out in the 3rd Round?

920. Town put this "United" out of the FA Cup after a 6th Round Replay in 1974-1975. Name them.

FINAL LEAGUE POSITIONS - 3

ALL YOU HAVE TO DO HERE IS ASSOCIATE TOWN WITH THEIR FINAL POSITION IN THE LEAGUE FOR THE SEASON MENTIONED (FOR EXAMPLE 1967-1968 Div 2 - ?)

921.	19671968	Div 2	8th
922.	1974-1975	Div 1	22nd
923.	1979-1980	Div 1	19th
924.	1981-1982	Div 1	18th
925.	1988-1989	Div 2	3rd
926.	1993-1994	Prem	4th
927.	1994-1995	Prem	5th
928.	1996-1997	Div 1	1st
929.	2000-2001	Prem	2nd
930.	2001-2002	Prem	3rd

THE LEAGUE CUP - 2

931. What Lancashire side put Town out of the League Cup in 1981-1982 and again in 1982-1983?

932. Town beat Manchester United 2-0 in the 3rd Round of the League Cup in season 1997-1998, but can you recall the name of either of their goalscorers?

933. This famous name of a Town player scored for Ipswich in the League Cup in 1974-1975 and in 2000-2001. Can you recall the name?

934. Up to the end of the 2004-2005 season, who is Town's all-time leading goalscorer in the League Cup?

935. Who was the Town Manager when they entered the League Cup for the first time?

936. What "Kevin" scored for Town against Leeds in the 1981-1982 League Cup?

937. Name either of Town's 2 goalscorers in their League Cup Semi-Final encounter with Liverpool in 1981-1982.

938. Can you name the player, whose Christian name and surname both begin with the same letter, who scored against Stockport County in Round 2 in 1995-1996?

939. This "Mick" scored for Town in 3 consecutive League Cup competitions from 1996-1997 to 1998-1999. Can you name him?

940. Up to the end of the 2004-2005 season, how many games, to the nearest 25, have Town played in the League Cup?

TRIVIA - 10

941. What "City" were the visitors in 1968 when the Match of the Day cameras visited Portman Road for the first time?

942. Against what country, beginning with the letter "A", did Ray Crawford score his only goal for England?

943. In what year was Joe Royle sacked as the Manager of Manchester City?

944. Can you recall the side that Town beat 6-1 in the 6th Round of the FA Cup on their way to winning the trophy in 1978?

945. Name the Town Manager who had a 1 in 3 win record during his time in charge with an overall record of Played: 231, Won:77, Drew: 75, Lost: 79, For: 291, Against: 308.

946. Against what "TSV" did Town play two friendlies during their successful 1961-1962 Championship winning season?

947. Can you name any 1 of the 3 English League sides that Town played in the Texaco Cup?

948. In August 1936, against what "Rangers" did Town play their first home game as a Professional club?

949. Up to the end of the 2004-2005 season, what is the highest number of consecutive draws put together by Town - 6, 8 or 10?

950. In what year did former Town boss, John Lyall, guide West Ham United to the European Cup Winners' Cup Final?

PLAYERS - 10

951. Up to the end of the 2004-2005 season only 2 players with surnames beginning with the letter "Y" have played Professional football for Town. Name them both.

952. Who scored both goals for Town in their League Championship clinching a 2-0 victory over Aston Villa at Portman Road on 28 April 1962?

953. What London club did Marcus Bent play for from January 1998 to January 1999?

954. What player left Town for Glasgow Celtic in July 1999?

955. This "Trevor" played for Town, Leyton Orient and Watford. Name him.

956. Can you recall the Dutch side that Romeo Zondervan joined when he left Town in 1992?

957. Can you name the former Ipswich captain who, during his spell as the Manager of Stoke City, paid Bury £40,000 for Lee Dixon?

958. What team did Roger Osborne join when he left Town?

959. Who did Town sign from Swindon Town in June 2005 for £450,000?

960. Apart from Tottenham Hotspur, what other London club did Alan Brazil play for?

LEADING GOALSCORERS
BY SEASON - 3

*AALL YOU HAVE TO DO HERE IS ASSOCIATE THE PLAYER WITH
THE SEASON HE WAS TOWN'S LEADING GOALSCORER*

961.	1969-1970	Eric Gates	16
962.	1973-1974	Trevor Whymark	15
963.	1976-1977	Chris Kiwomya	19
964.	1977-1978	Marcus Stewart	21
965.	1980-1981	Ian Marshall	15
966.	1983-1984	Kevin Wilson	15
967.	1985-1986	Colin Viljoen	6
968.	1991-1992	John Wark	36
969.	1993-1994	Paul Mariner	22
970.	2000-2001	Bryan Hamilton	19

SCORING DEBUTANTS - 2

ALL YOU HAVE TO DO HERE IS ASSOCIATE THE PLAYER WITH THE TEAM HE SCORED AGAINST ON HIS TOWN DEBUT

971. Neil Midgley   Stoke City

972. Gary Croft   Arsenal

973. Kevin Wilson   Leicester City

974. Paul Mason   Southampton

975. David Johnson   Manchester City

976. Alex Mathie   Watford

977. Adam Tanner   West Bromwich Albion

978. Mark Stuart   Gillingham

979. Sergei Baltacha   Wolverhampton Wanderers

980. Keith Bertschin   Oldham Athletic

RAY CRAWFORD

981.   In what year did Ray arrive at Portman Road for the first of his 2 spells with the club - 1958, 1959 or 1960?

982.   Following on from Q981, can you name the South Coast side that Ray played for before he joined Town?

983.   Against what Welsh "City" did he make his first debut for Town?

984.   To the nearest 5, how many full International caps did he win for England?

985.   What "Wanderers" did Ray sign for when he first left Portman Road?

986.   To the nearest 5, how many League goals did Ray score for Town during their Division 2 Championship winning season in 1960-1961?

987.   In what year did he leave Ipswich to join the team in Q985 - 1963, 1964 or 1965?

988.   Can you recall the "United" where Ray ended his career?

989.   What London club did Ray sign for in March 1969?

990.   Against what club, a former club of Ray's, did he make his last appearance for Town?

JOHN WARK - 2

991.   In what year did John sign for Town during the second of his three spells at Portman Road?

992.   To the nearest 5, how many European appearances did John make for Town during his playing career?

993.   Following on from Q992, how many goals did he score for Town in Europe - 18, 19 or 20?

994.   Can you recall the name of the club that John left to sign for Town for the third time during his career?

995.   Name the Manager who signed John for Liverpool in March 1984.

996.   To the nearest £50,000, how much did Town receive from Liverpool for John?

997.   What Professional "Award" did he win in 1981?

998.   Against what club did he score on his debut for Liverpool - Arsenal, Queens Park Rangers or Watford?

999.   How many League Championship medals did he win during his career?

1000. With what "Paul" did he manage Town for 3 games after the departure of John Lyall?

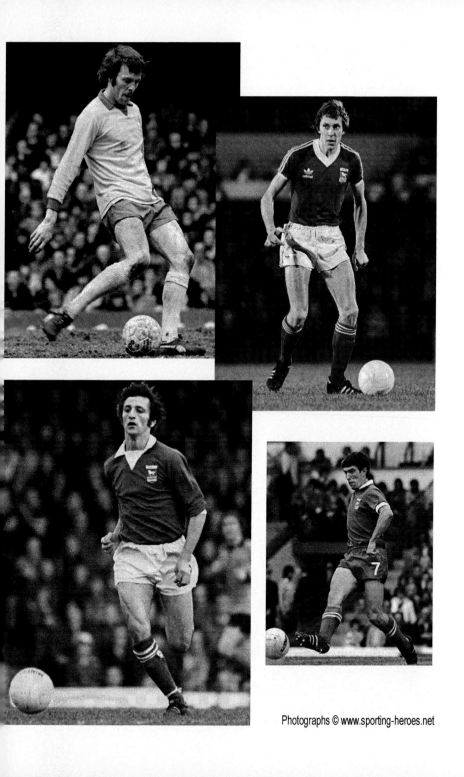

MARCUS BENT

1001. In what year did Marcus arrive at Portman Road - 1999,2000 or 2001?

1002. Can you name the "Rovers" he played for before he joined Ipswich?

1003. Against what North East Premier League club did he make his debut for Town?

1004. To the nearest £250,000, how much did he cost Town?

1005. What "City" did he join on loan in September 2003?

1006. To the nearest 5, how many goals did he score for Town during his time at Portman Road?

1007. Can you recall the club he signed for in June 2004?

1008. Following on from Q1007, to the nearest £50,000, how much did Town receive for him?

1009. At what London area club, nicknamed 'The Bees', did Marcus begin his football career?

1010. What "United" did he play for prior to joining the team in Q1002?

UNLUCKY KEEPERS

1011.   Can you name the Town goalkeeper who was replaced at half time in the home game against Reading on 28 September 2004.

1012.   Following on from Q1011, who replaced him in goal?

1013.   Who was in goal for Ipswich when Manchester United beat them 9-0 at Old Trafford in a Premier League game on 4 March 1995?

1014.   Name the goalkeeper who was sent off for bringing down Leicester City's Robbie Savage in an away game on 8th September 2001.

1015.   Which outfield player took over temporarily in goal for Richard Wright in Town's 5-2 home win over Oxford United on 24 February 1998?

1016.   Against what "Town" was Richard Wright carried off in a 3-1 home defeat on 7 September 1996?

1017.   Neil Gregory took over in goal in Q1016, but can you name the future Town striker who scored against Ipswich in the game?

1018.   Name the "Jack" who was replaced in goal by Town winger James Gaynor on two separate occasions during the 1952-1953 season.

1019.   Can you recall the Ipswich goalkeeper who injured his hand in a 1-1 draw with Leeds United on 7 April 1979 and was replaced in goal by Town winger, Clive Woods?

1020.   Who made his Town debut when he came on as substitute after only 2 minutes in a 0-0 draw on 26 September 1992?

JOHN LYALL

1021. In what year did John take charge at Portman Road?

1022. What club did John manage prior to becoming the Ipswich Manager?

1023. Can you recall Town's Yorkshire opponents for John's first game in charge of the club?

1024. Can you recall how many years John was in charge of the team in Q1022 - 14, 15 or 16?

1025. How many times did John win the FA Cup as a Manager?

1026. Following on from Q1025, name any year in which he guided a team to FA Cup glory.

1027. What was the highest ever League position to which John managed a team to in the First Division?

1028. Following on from Q1027, in what season did this take place - 1984-1985, 1985-1986 or 1986-1987?

1029. What was the only trophy that Town won under his management?

1030. In what year did Ipswich lift the trophy in Q1029?

SEASON 1981-1982
LEAGUE RUNNERS-UP

1031.   Name the Scottish team that Town beat 2-1 in a pre-season friendly away game.

1032.   Can you recall the North East club that Town drew 3-3 with at Portman Road on the opening day of the season?

1033.   What Brazilian side did Town beat 2-1 in Barcelona's Nou Camp Stadium in a pre-season friendly?

1034.   Name the Scottish club that were the first team to beat Town during the 1981-1982 season.

1035.   Name the Town striker who was the club's highest League goalscorer during the 1981-1982 season with 22 goals.

1036.   Who, along with the player in Q1035, was Town's highest leading goalscorer in Cup competitions for the season with 6 goals?

1037.   Town ended the season in Runners-Up position in the First Division. Who were crowned Champions?

1038.   What London club did Town beat 2-1 at Portman Road on the last day of the season?

1039.   To the nearest 10, how many League points did Town have at the end of the season?

1040.   By how many points did the team in Q1039 win the Championship over Town?

IPSWICH TOWN v.
MANCHESTER UNITED - 2

1041. Up to the end of the 2004-2005 season, who was the last Town Manager to record a win over United?

1042. Following on from Q1041, name any Town goalscorer in the game.

1043. To the nearest 10,000, what is the highest attendance in a meeting between the 2 sides?

1044. Who lies in second place behind Paul Mariner with 4 goals as overall highest scorer for Town against United?

1045. To the nearest 10, how many times have the 2 clubs met in a competitive fixture up to the end of the 2004-2005 season?

1046. Who scored both goals in Town's 2-1 win over United during Bobby Robson's last game in charge of a Town v. United game?

1047. Name the future United player who scored for Town in their 2-1 win at Old Trafford on 5 September 1981.

1048. Who scored a famous hat-trick for Town in a 6-0 win over United at Portman Road on 1 March 1980?

1049. Following on from Q1048, can you name the United goalkeeper, capped by England at International level, who saved 2 penalties in the game?

1050. What "Ted" scored Town's first ever goal against United when Ipswich beat them 4-1 at Portman Road in a Division One game on 18 November 1961?

ALL-TIME LEADING
GOALSCORERS - 2

ALL YOU HAVE TO DO HERE IS ASSOCIATE THE PLAYER WITH
THE NUMBER OF GOALS HE SCORED FOR TOWN IN HIS CAREER

1051.	Paul Mariner	54
1052.	David Johnson	56
1053.	Ted Phillips	45
1054.	Jason Dozzell	69
1055.	Trevor Whymark	62
1056.	Gerard Baker	179
1057.	Colin Viljoen	135
1058.	Mick Lambert	66
1059.	Simon Milton	73
1060.	Frank Brogan	104

KEVIN BEATTIE

1061. In what year did Kevin sign as a Professional for Town - 1970, 1971 or 1972?

1062. Can you name the "United" against which Kevin made his debut for Town?

1063. To the nearest 50, how many appearances did Kevin make during his Town career?

1064. What "United" did Kevin join when he left Ipswich?

1065. In what year did Kevin leave Ipswich Town - 1981, 1982 or 1983?

1066. How many full International appearances did he make for England - 9, 10 or 11?

1067. Can you recall the year in which he made his full International debut for England - 1974, 1975 or 1976?

1068. Following on from Q1067, England beat Cyprus 5-0 at Wembley in a European Championships qualifying game. Who scored all 5 of England's goals in the game?

1069. Which one of the "Home" countries was the only one against which Kevin scored a goal for England in the games he played in Q1066?

1070. What was Kevin's nickname during his playing days at Town?

DAVID JOHNSON

1071. In what year did David join Ipswich - 1971, 1972 or 1973?

1072. From what Merseyside club did David join Town?

1073. To the nearest 5, how many full International caps did he win for England?

1074. What team did David sign for when he left Portman Road?

1075. To the nearest 10, how many goals did David score for Town during his time at Portman Road?

1076. In what year did he leave Ipswich to join the team in Q1074?

1077. Can you recall the "City" he signed for in March 1984, making 6 appearances for them (2 as a substitute), scoring once?

1078. What "hard sounding" North American Soccer League team did he move to in 1984?

1079. Against what "United" did he make his debut for Town in a First Division game?

1080. To the nearest 50, how many appearances did he make for Town?

TED PHILLIPS

1081.   In what year did Ted arrive at Portman Road - 1952, 1953 or
        1954?

1082.   Apart from Ipswich, what other "Town" did Ted play for in the
        Football League?

1083.   Against what club, nicknamed 'The Hornets', did he make his
        debut for Town?

1084.   Can you name the former Manchester United Manager who first
        spotted Ted and signed him for Town?

1085.   What "United" did Ted sign for in September 1965?

1086.   To the nearest 50, how many appearances did he make for Town?

1087.   During his career he took 22 penalties. How many of them did he
        miss?

1088.   Prior to taking up football for a living, in what "outdoor" trade
        did Ted complete a 4-year apprenticeship?

1089.   Can you name the London area team that Ted signed for in March
        1964?

1090.   To the nearest 25, how many goals did Ted score for Town
        during his time at Portman Road?

TOWN AT WEMBLEY

1091. How many times did Town play at Wembley Stadium?

1092. In what year did Town first play at Wembley - 1918, 1928 or 1938?

1093. In what "League" did Town play Ealing Association in the game in Q1092?

1094. What team is the only team that Town met in an FA Cup Final at the Twin Towers?

1095. Can you recall the only team Town have played in the FA Charity Shield game at Wembley?

1096. In what year did Town last take to the Wembley turf?

1097. Following on from Q1096, what Yorkshire side were the opposition?

1098. Who was the last player to score a goal for Ipswich Town at the Twin Towers?

1099. To the nearest 5, how many players actually played for Town at Wembley Stadium?

1100. Who is the only player to have captained Town twice at Wembley?

TOWN AT THE MOVIES

1101.   What was the name of the movie about a football match involving The Allies and Germany, that John Wark starred in during the early 1980s?

1102.   How many Ipswich Town players (past or present at the time the movie was made), starred in the movie in Q1101?

1103.   Following on from Q1102, name any 3 of them.

1104.   Can you recall the name of any Manchester City player (past or present at the time the movie was made), that starred in the movie in Q1101?

1105.   Can you recall the 1979 movie in which Portman Road was used as a venue for an FA Cup Semi-Final?

1106.   Following on from Q1105, can you name the famous British actress that wrote the Screenplay or the British actor, who played Judas Iscariot in "Jesus of Nazareth", who played the lead role in the movie?

1107.   Name both the 1966 World Cup winner and the 1970 World Cup winner who starred in the movie in Q1101.

1108.   "Do you know" the name of the famous British actor that played Captain John Colby in the movie in Q1101?

1109.   Name the American actor, better known for his movie roles in another sport, who played in goal for the Allies.

1110.   This Argentinean World Cup winner played for the Allies in the movie in Q1101. Can you name him?

ALLAN HUNTER

1111. In what year did Allan sign for Town - 1970, 1971 or 1972?

1112. From what "Rovers" did Town sign Allan?

1113. Can you recall the Irish team where he began his career - Cliftonville, Coleraine or Crusaders?

1114. To the nearest 10, how many full International caps did he win with Northern Ireland?

1115. In what year, during the early 1980s, did Allan leave Town?

1116. How many goals did he score for Town during his career - 10, 15 or 20?

1117. Name the "City" against which he made his Town debut.

1118. Can you recall the "Town" he played against in his final game for Ipswich Town?

1119. What "Athletic" did Allan play for prior to signing for the team in Q1112?

1120. Name the 'United' Allan joined when he left Portman Road.

THE 1990s

1121.   Who was appointed Town Manager in season 1990-1991?

1122.   In Town's first season in the FA Premier League they completed a League Double over Norwich City. Can you recall either the home or away score?

1123.   This Second Division Welsh team put Town out of the FA Cup in 1994-1995. Name them.

1124.   On the last day of the 1995-1996 season Town needed a win to clinch a Play-Off space. What London team held them to a 0-0 score at Portman Road to deny them a Play-Off spot?

1125.   Can you recall the Town player who was sold in the 1998-1999 close season for £6 million?

1126.   Who took charge of Town in January 1995 after John Lyall resigned?

1127.   In what season did Town just miss relegation from the FA Premier League thanks to Chelsea's win over Sheffield United on the final day of the season when Mark Stein scored in the last minute of the game?

1128.   Against what "United" did Town's 1-1 away draw clinch the Division 2 Championship for them in season 1991-1992?

1129.   Who was voted Town's "Player of the Year" in season 1991-1992?

1130.   Name the team that Town lost to in the 1997-1998 Play-Offs for promotion to the FA Premier League.

JOHN DUNCAN

1131. In what year was John appointed the Manager of Ipswich Town?

1132. What Midlands club did Town play in John's first competitive game in charge of the club?

1133. Can you recall the year he left Town?

1134. Name the Midlands club Town played in John's last game in charge of the club.

1135. What Scottish club signed him when he was just 17 - Celtic, Dundee or Falkirk?

1136. John joined a London club in 1974. Name them.

1137. Following on from Q1136, to the nearest £50,000, how much did they pay for him?

1138. What "County" did he sign for in 1978?

1139. What "United" was John once the Player/Manager of?

1140. Can you recall the club he guided to the Fourth Division Championship?

MIXED BAG

1141. Can you name the overseas Professional snooker player who wore an Ipswich Town tie during a televised tournament in 1978?

1142. Apart from Manchester City and Bristol City, what other "City" did Joe Royle play for during his career?

1143. Up to the end of the 2004-2005 season, what is the highest number of consecutive games played by Town without recording a draw - 24, 26 or 28?

1144. Against what "Athletic" did Marcus Bent play his last game for Town?

1145. Can you recall the "City" that Town played when John Lyall managed the team for the last time?

1146. What team were Town playing in front of a crowd of 100,000 on 21 March 1979?

1147. Who was Town's leading goalscorer during the 2003-2004 season with 16 goals?

1148. Can you name the player who is Town's all-time leading goalscorer with 227 goals for the club?

1149. Up to the end of the 2004-2005 season, to the nearest 25, how many own goals has Town benefited from?

1150. Peter Beardsley and a former Town hero share the distinction of scoring winning Derby goals for both Merseyside clubs. Name the former Town striker.

JIM MAGILTON

1151. In what year did Jim make his debut for Ipswich Town?

1152. From what Yorkshire club did Town sign Jim?

1153. Can you recall the Lancashire club where Jim began his career as an Apprentice?

1154. Name the team with an "X" in their name that Jim signed for when he left the team in Q1153.

1155. Where in Northern Ireland was Jim born - Belfast, Coleraine or Lisburn?

1156. Can you recall the South Coast club he joined after leaving the team in Q1154?

1157. How much, to the nearest £300,000 did the team in Q1152 pay for Jim's services?

1158. Against what North East club did Jim make his debut for Town?

1159. What season has been Jim's most productive at Portman Road in terms of goals scored, with 7?

1160. To the nearest £200,000, how much did Town pay for Jim?

GEORGE BURLEY

1161.   In what year did George sign for Ipswich Town - 1971, 1972 or 1973?

1162.   What North East club did George sign for when he left Portman Road?

1163.   Can you recall the "United" against which he made his Town debut in a Division One away game?

1164.   Name the team George signed for when he left the team in Q1162.

1165.   How many full International caps did he win with Scotland - 11, 21 or 31?

1166.   In what year was George appointed the Manager of Ipswich Town?

1167.   What team did he manage during the 2004-2005 season?

1168.   In what year did George guide Town to the FA Premier League after a Play-Off Final victory at Wembley?

1169.   After their first season in the FA Premier League under George's management, Town qualified for the UEFA Cup. Prior to this, when was the last season Town played in the UEFA Cup?

1170.   Can you recall the "United" where George ended his playing career from August 1994 to December 1994?

THE 1960's

1171. In what year did Sir Alf Ramsey lead England to World Cup glory?

1172. What "Colin" scored a hat-trick on his debut for Town against Portsmouth at home on 25th March 1967?

1173. Following on from Q1172, can you name the famous Town striker who also scored in Ipswich's 4-2 win?

1174. What did Town win in season 1960-1961?

1175. Following on from Q1174, against what "United" did Town record a notable double winning 5-2 away and 4-0 at home?

1176. In what season did Town set their record home victory, a 7-0 win over Portsmouth?

1177. In season 1968-1969 what Midlands club did former Town Manager, Bill McGarry, take the Manager's job at?

1178. In what season did Town win the Second Division Championship for the second time during the 1960s?

1179. Can you recall the "City" that Town were 2 goals down to after only 30 minutes on 3rd February 1968 in an away League game only to finish the game 4-3 winners?

1180. Name the "Gerry" who was Town's leading goal scorer in season 1963-1964 with 18 goals.

SIMON MILTON

1181.   In what year did Simon join Town - 1987, 1988 or 1989?

1182.   What club did Simon sign for when he left Town?

1183.   To the nearest "50", how many League appearances did he make for Town?

1184.   From what "Town" did Town sign Simon?

1185.   How much did Simon cost Town - £5,500, £55,500 0r £100,500?

1186.   Can you recall the "United" he joined after leaving the team in Q1182?

1187.   In what year during the late 1990's did he leave Portman Road?

1188.   To the nearest "10", how many goals did he score for Town?

1189.   Why did he leave Town - free transfer, injury or retirement?

1190.   Can you recall the "Town" Ipswich played when he made his debut for the club?

UP FOR THE CUP

1191. What club, and future FA Premier League Champions, put Town out of the FA Cup in 1967-1968?

1192. Name the London club Town beat 3-0 in the 4th Round of the FA Cup at Portman Road on 29th January 1994?

1193. Name the "City" Town beat 3-2 away in the 4th Round of the Full Members Cup in season 1986-1987 to book their Semi-Final appearance.

1194. Following on from Q1193, name any scorer for Town in the game.

1195. How many Replays did Town have to play in the FA Cup during the 1970-1971 season?

1196. · Apart from the FA Cup, Full Members Cup and League Cup, what other "medical sounding" Cup did Town play in during the 1988-1989 season?

1197. Name any Town goal scorer in their 3-0 away FA Cup 3rd Round victory over Morecambe on 6th January 2001.

1198. Town won the FA Cup in 1978 but what "Wanderers" put them out of the Cup the previous season?

1199. What "Albion" put Town out of the 1976-1977 League Cup after a Replay in the 2nd Round?

1200. Prior to winning the UEFA Cup in 1981, what Swiss Team put Town out of the 1979-1980 UEFA Cup?

ANSWERS

THE HISTORY - 1

1. 1878
2. Leeds United
3. Mick Mills
4. 1 (1961-1962)
5. Turned Professional
6. The Southern League
7. 30,300
8. Semi-Final (in 1981-1982, 1984-1985 & 2000-2001)
9. Kieron Dyer
10. 7-0

SEASON 2001-2002

11. 18th
12. Derby County
13. Finidi George (Richard Naylor also scored)
14. Manchester United (at Old Trafford)
15. Marcus Bent
16. Jamie Clapham (at Bolton) & Darren Bent (home to Boro)
17. Arsenal
18. 36
19. Charlton Athletic
20. Liverpool

MICK MILLS - 1

21. 1965
22. Southampton
23. 732
24. Portsmouth
25. 42
26. Stoke City
27. 1982
28. 1982 (in Spain)
29. Ron Greenwood
30. Birmingham City

TRIVIA - 1

31. Bristol City
32. 2
33. Millwall (in Division 3 South)
34. Shefki Kuqi
35. Steve McCall
36. Foggia
37. Birmingham City (4-0 away on 8 September 1954 & 2-1 at home on 15 September 1954)
38. Ted Phillips (41 in Division 3 South, 1956-1957)
39. The Division 3 South Championship in 1953-1954
40. Portsmouth

COMINGS AND GOINGS - 1

41. Titus Bramble   to Newcastle United
42. John Deehan   from Norwich City
43. George Burley   to Sunderland
44. Frank Clarke   from Queens Park Rangers
45. Alan Brazil   to Tottenham Hotspur
46. Paul Goddard   from Millwall
47. Marcus Bent   to Everton
48. Chris Bart-Williams   from Charlton Athletic
49. Terry Butcher   to Glasgow Rangers
50. Bryan Hamilton   from Linfield

THE 1980s - 1

51. John Wark
52. Charlton Athletic
53. Jason Dozzell
54. Frans Thijssen & Paul Mariner
55. Roma
56. Frank Yallop
57. Sergei Baltacha
58. Eric Gates
59. 1985-1986
60. Bobby Ferguson

DERBY DAYS: IPSWICH TOWN v. NORWICH CITY - 1

61. John Wark (29 between 1977 and 1996)
62. 3
63. Trevor Whymark

64.	Mick Lambert
65.	The Full Members Cup
66.	Andy Marshall
67.	Ray Crawford
68.	1992-1993 (at Carrow Road on 21 December 1992)
69.	Justin Fashanu
70.	Joe Royle

PLAYERS - 1

71.	Kevin Beattie
72.	RCD Mallorca
73.	Richard Naylor
74.	£4,500,000
75.	Swansea City
76.	Kevin Wilson
77.	John Deehan
78.	Matt Richards
79.	Darren Bent
80.	Tommy Miller (Hartlepool United)

BLUES' PLAYER OF THE YEAR - 1

81.	2003-2004	Ian Westlake
82.	1999-2000	James Scowcroft
83.	1997-1998	Matt Holland
84.	1994-1995	Craig Forrest
85.	1992-1993	Mick Stockwell
86.	1989-1990	John Wark
87.	1985-1986	Terry Butcher
88.	1978-1979	Arnold Muhren
89.	1975-1976	Allan Hunter
90.	1972-1973	Kevin Beattie

UEFA CUP WINNERS - 1

91.	1981
92.	Mick Mills
93.	AZ 67 Alkmaar
94.	Aris Salonika
95.	14
96.	Terry Butcher
97.	St Etienne
98.	2

99. Johnny Metgod
100. Michel Platini (he captained France to European Championship success in 1984)

FINAL LEAGUE POSITIONS - 1

101.	1961-1962	Div 1	1st
102.	1968-1969	Div 1	12th
103.	1973-1974	Div 1	4th
104.	1978-1979	Div 1	6th
105.	1982-1983	Div 1	9th
106.	1986-1987	Div 2	5th
107.	1992-1993	Prem	16th
108.	1995-1996	Div 1	7th
109.	1997-1998	Div 1	5th
110.	1999-2000	Div 1	3rd

PENALTY SHOOT-OUTS

111. 7
112. Lokomotive Leipzig
113. Kevin Beattie, Brian Talbot & Trevor Whymark
114. 1
115. Chelsea
116. Peter Morris
117. Craig Forrest
118. Barcelona
119. Liverpool
120. Armstrong, Holland, Magilton & Miller

SIR ALF RAMSEY - 1

121. 1955 (on 8 August)
122. Torquay United (Town lost 2-0 at home on 20 August 1955)
123. Southampton
124. Tottenham Hotspur
125. The Division 3 South Championship (1957)
126. 1962
127. 1966
128. 369
129. Birmingham City
130. 1963

SIR BOBBY ROBSON
131. Ron Greenwood
132. 20
133. 1957 (27 November v. France)
134. 1978 (on 6 May at Wembley Stadium)
135. Fulham
136. Middlesbrough
137. PSV Eindhoven
138. Vancouver Whitecaps
139. Sweden 1958
140. West Bromwich Albion

TOWN AT THE WORLD CUP FINALS
141. 2
142. Matt Holland (Republic of Ireland) & Amir Karic (Slovenia)
143. Terry Butcher
144. Bontcho Guentchev (Bulgaria)
145. John Wark (for Scotland in the 29th minute v. New Zealand at the 1982 Finals in Spain)
146. 4 (1982, 1986, 1994 & 2002 - Terry Butcher was a Glasgow Rangers player in 1990)
147. Terry Butcher, Paul Mariner & Mick Mills (England) and Alan Brazil, George Burley & John Wark (Scotland)
148. John Wark (3 goals from 2 appearances in 1982)
149. Mick Mills (for England at the 1982 Finals in Spain)
150. France (England won 3-1 in Estadio San Mamés)

SQUAD NUMBERS 2004-2005 - 1
151.	Lewis Price	No. 34
152.	Jimmy Juan	No. 19
153.	Richard Naylor	No. 6
154.	Pablo Counago	No. 9
155.	Ian Westlake	No. 33
156.	Scott Mitchell	No. 21
157.	Dean Bowditch	No. 17
158.	Jason De Vos	No. 4
159.	Owen Garvan	No. 23
160.	Shefki Kuqi	No. 32

SEASON 2003-2004 - 1

161. Levski Sofia
162. Kidderminster Harriers (won 1-0)
163. Tommy Miller (in a 1-1 home draw on the opening day of the season)
164. Walsall
165. Pablo Counago
166. Darren Bent
167. West Ham United
168. Cardiff City
169. 5th
170. Norwich City

TRIVIA - 2

171. John Duncan
172. The official opening of Kettering Town's new floodlight system (2-2 draw on 9 October 1961)
173. 2
174. 9 (28 November 1981 to 3 January 1982)
175. Trevor Putney
176. 2 (1982-1983 & 1983-1984)
177. Crystal Palace
178. Norwich City (away in the First Division)
179. 38,010 (v. Leeds United on 8 March 1975, FA Cup 6th Round)
180. Slovan Liberec

PLAYERS - 2

181. Keith Bertschin
182. Jack (1963-1966) & Ron (1965-1968)
183. Leeds United
184. Birmingham City (from) & Leicester City (to)
185. Romeo Zondervan
186. Richard Naylor
187. Middlesbrough (March 1995)
188. Paul Mariner
189. Tommy Miller
190. Kevin Beattie

SEASON 2004-2005 - 1

191. Newcastle United
192. Doncaster Rovers
193. Richard Naylor (in a 2-1 home win over Gillingham on the opening day of

the season)
194.   Derby County (3-2 away on 14 August 2004)
195.   Tommy Miller
196.   Wigan Athletic (Coca-Cola Championship Runners-Up)
197.   Queens Park Rangers
198.   Stoke City
199.   Bolton Wanderers
200.   West Ham United

PABLO COUNAGO

201.   Spanish (born in Redondela, Pontevedra, Spain on 9 August 1979)
202.   2001 (July)
203.   Real Celta Vigo
204.   Free Transfer
205.   Sunderland (away in the FA Barclaycard Premiership on 18 August 2001)
206.   Numancia
207.   Huelva
208.   20
209.   Real Celta Vigo
210.   Leicester City (he scored twice in a 6-1 home win on 18th August 2002)

TERRY BUTCHER

211.   1978 (on 15 April away to Everton in Division One)
212.   Glasgow Rangers
213.   271
214.   Singapore (on 28 December 1958)
215.   77
216.   Coventry City
217.   Sweden (6 September 1989 - Rasunda Stadium, Stockholm)
218.   1990 (as a stand-in captain)
219.   Sunderland
220.   Motherwell

LEADING GOALSCORERS BY SEASON - 1

221.	1968-1969	John O'Rourke	17
222.	1972-1973	Trevor Whymark	16
223.	1974-1975	Bryan Hamilton	17
224.	1978-1979	Paul Mariner	17
225.	1981-1982	Alan Brazil	28
226.	1984-1985	Eric Gates	16
227.	1987-1988	David Lowe	18

228.	1988-1989	Dalian Atkinson	13
229.	1996-1997	Paul Mason	14
230.	2001-2002	Marcus Bent	10

CUP COMPETITIONS - 1

231. The Texaco Cup (won both games played)
232. 3 (Won: 0, Drew: 1, Lost: 2)
233. The Division 3 South (North) Cup
234. Gerd Muller
235. Frans Thijssen
236. Mick Mills
237. Luton Town
238. Andy Marshall
239. Notts County
240. They beat Arsenal 1-0 in the Final and won their Semi-Final tie at Arsenal's ground

IPSWICH TOWN v. MANCHESTER UNITED - 1

241. 1958 (Town lost 2-0 at Old Trafford on 25 January)
242. The FA Cup (1957-1958 season)
243. Kevin Beattie (his only goal for Town against United)
244. 1997 (League Cup 3rd Round, 2-0 win at Portman Road)
245. Fabian Wilnis (1-1 home draw on 22 August 2000)
246. Bobby Robson
247. John Duncan
248. Chris Kiwomya (in a 1-1 draw at Old Trafford on 22 August 1992)
249. Paul Mariner
250. Jackie Milburn (Newcastle United & England)

SEASON 2002-2003 - 1

251. 7th
252. Leicester City
253. Pablo Counago & Matt Holland
254. Watford
255. Middlesbrough (3-1 at Portman Road on 6 November)
256. Darren Bent, Matt Holland & Jim Magilton (plus a Derby County own goal)
257. Portsmouth
258. 70
259. Pablo Counago (20 goals in all competitions)
260. Leicester City

TRIVIA - 3

261. Ernest
262. 2-2 (Town won the Replay 3-0)
263. The Poppy Fund (Town won 5-2 on 6 November 1961)
264. The League Cup
265. 23 (28 August 1963 to 14 December 1963)
266. Birmingham City
267. The Football League
268. George Burley
269. Spain (in Spain on 5 July 1982)
270. Sunderland (2-1 at Portman Road)

PLAYERS - 3

271. Alan Mullery (v. Yugoslavia on 5 June 1968)
272. Jimmy Robertson (on 7 September 1971 in a 3-1 home defeat, Round 2)
273. Mick Mills, Brian Talbot & John Wark
274. Bryan Hamilton
275. 2
276. Richard Naylor
277. Paul Mariner
278. John Wark
279. David Linighan
280. Dean Bowditch

BRYAN HAMILTON

281. 1971 (August)
282. Linfield
283. Everton (at home in Division 1 on 14 August 1971)
284. 199 (includes 13 as substitute)
285. Everton
286. Northern Ireland
287. 50 (21 whilst at Town)
288. Millwall (July 1977)
289. Swindon Town (November 1978 to October 1980)
290. Tranmere Rovers

THE 1970s - 1

291. Bill Baxter
292. The FA Youth Cup & The Texaco Cup
293. 3rd
294. Barcelona

295.   1974-1975
296.   The Daily Express 5-a-side Championships
297.   Manchester United (lost 1-0 to Southampton)
298.   Trevor Whymark
299.   Arsenal
300.   Allan Hunter (Ipswich Town & Northern Ireland)

SEASON 1992-1993
FIRST SEASON IN THE PREMIER LEAGUE

301.   Aston Villa (1-1 at home on 15 August 1992)
302.   Gavin Johnson (in the game in Q301)
303.   Wimbledon (1-0 away on 18 August 1992)
304.   16th
305.   Chris Kiwomya (10 League, 7 Cups)
306.   John Lyall
307.   Wigan Athletic (2-2 away & 4-0 at home)
308.   Arsenal
309.   12 (Won: 12, Drew: 16, Lost: 14)
310.   Frank Yallop (1-1 at Portman Road on 9th August 1992)

BOBBY FERGUSON

311.   1982
312.   Bobby Robson
313.   Brighton & Hove Albion
314.   1971
315.   Youth Team Coach
316.   9th (1982-1983)
317.   1985-1986 (finished 20th)
318.   258 (210 League & 48 Cup/Play-Offs)
319.   1987
320.   Charlton Athletic (in a 2-1 away defeat in the Division 1/2 Play-Off
        Semi-Final on 17 May 1987)

TOWN IN EUROPE - 1

321.   1962-1963
322.   Mick Mills (40)
323.   62
324.   The UEFA Cup (52)
325.   Undefeated at home
326.   Barcelona (33,663 in the UEFA Cup on 23 October 1977)
327.   John Wark

328. Matt Holland (10)
329. 39
330. The Quarter-Finals

THE UEFA CUP
331. Falcao
332. Lokomotive Leipzig
333. FC Twente
334. Aberdeen
335. Gordon Strachan (Coventry City & Southampton)
336. FC Bruges
337. Torpedo Moscow
338. Grasshoppers Zurich
339. Inter Milan
340. Ronaldo

FULL MEMBERS CUP - 1
341. 1985
342. English clubs were banned from playing in Europe
343. 1986-1987
344. Plymouth Argyle
345. Semi-Finals
346. John Duncan (1987-1988, 1988-1989 & 1989-1990)
347. Chelsea
348. David Gregory
349. 6
350. ZDS

TRIVIA - 4
351. Sheffield United (9 - 6 Sheffield United & 3 Town)
352. Walthamstow Avenue (1-0 away on 16th December after a 2-2 home draw
4 days earlier)
353. 71 (Drew:53, Lost: 86)
354. 5th (season 2003-2004)
355. 2 (1953-1954 & 1956-1957)
356. Coventry City (in Division 3 South)
357. Sheffield United (4-0 on 3rd March) & Sheffield Wednesday (2-1 on
9 March)
358. Oxford United (Round 4)
359. A floodlight failure
360. 1994 (December)

PLAYERS - 4

361. Ray Crawford
362. £450,000
363. Blackpool
364. Eric Gates
365. Dalian Atkinson
366. Marcus Bent
367. Terry Austin
368. David Lowe
369. Ted Phillips
370. Alan Brazil Racing Club (or Alan Brazil Racing)

IPSWICH IN THE FA CUP - 1

371. Liverpool
372. Carlisle United (FA Cup 3rd Round, 1978-1979)
373. Tottenham Hotspur
374. Cardiff City (3-2 away in the 3rd Round)
375. Wolverhampton Wanderers
376. Mick Hill
377. Southampton (1976 FA Cup winners)
378. Morecambe
379. Manchester City
380. Blackburn Rovers (FA Premier League Champions in 1994-1995)

BLUES' PLAYER OF THE YEAR - 2

381.	2002-2003	Matt Holland
382.	2000-2001	Marcus Stewart
383.	1996-1997	Mauricio Taricco
384.	1991-1992	John Wark
385.	1986-1987	Romeo Zondervan
386.	1984-1985	Terry Butcher
387.	1983-1984	Trevor Putney
388.	1980-1981	Paul Cooper
389.	1976-1977	George Burley
390.	1973-1974	Kevin Beattie

JOHN WARK - 1

391. Glasgow (on 4 August 1957)
392. Leeds United
393. 1975 (on 27 March)
394. 539 (including 6 as substitute)

395.	1984 (March)
396.	Liverpool
397.	29
398.	£100,000
399.	Middlesbrough
400.	3

COMINGS AND GOINGS - 2

401.	Darren Ambrose	to Newcastle United
402.	Jason Cundy	from Tottenham Hotspur
403.	David Johnson	to Liverpool
404.	Kevin O'Callaghan	from Millwall
405.	David Geddis	to Aston Villa
406.	Tony Mowbray	from Glasgow Celtic
407.	Arnold Muhren	to Manchester United
408.	Mick Mills	from Portsmouth
409.	Russell Osman	to Leicester City
410.	Paul Mariner	from Plymouth Argyle

PORTMAN ROAD

411.	Preston North End
412.	An Army Training Camp
413.	Floodlights
414.	The retractable players' tunnel
415.	The first English all-seater stadium
416.	Billy Graham
417.	The Centre Spot Restaurant
418.	Rats
419.	Whippet Racing
420.	Match of the Day

CUP COMPETITIONS - 2

421.	1 (1995-1996)
422.	Vehicle Hire
423.	Wolverhampton Wanderers
424.	4 (season 1962-1963)
425.	Wimbledon
426.	John Wark (32nd minute in the Final, 2nd Leg)
427.	Tommy Miller, Richard Naylor & Martijn Reuser
428.	Bontcho Guentchev (for Bulgaria at the 1994 Finals in the USA)
429.	Amir Karic (for Slovenia against Spain on 2 June 2002)

430.   St Johnstone

SEASON 1980-1981
SO NEAR, YET SO FAR

431.   PSV Eindhoven (on 8 August)
432.   Leicester City
433.   John Wark
434.   Brighton & Hove Albion (0-1 at Albion on 11 November)
435.   Alan Brazil
436.   John Wark
437.   Aston Villa
438.   Southampton
439.   56
440.   4 (Villa had 60 points)

FINAL LEAGUE POSITIONS - 2

441.	1962-1963	Div 1	17th
442.	1965-1966	Div 2	15th
443.	1969-1970	Div 1	18th
444.	1972-1973	Div 1	4th
445.	1976-1977	Div 1	3rd
446.	1980-1981	Div 1	2nd
447.	1983-1984	Div 1	12th
448.	1985-1986	Div 1	20th
449.	1991-1992	Div 2	1st
450.	1998-1999	Div 1	3rd

TRIVIA - 5

451.   Cambridge United & Colchester United
452.   18th
453.   1999
454.   Belfast (on 31 December 1946)
455.   Sammy Chung
456.   10 (4 September 1954 to 16 October 1954)
457.   Division 3 South
458.   The 1974 World Cup Finals
459.   Nigel Havers
460.   Villa Park

PLAYERS - 5

461. Ian Redford
462. John Wark
463. Paul Mariner (in Town's 6-1 win over Millwall in the 6th Round)
464. Bryan Hamilton
465. Tommy Miller
466. Mick Mills and Russell Osman
467. George Burley
468. Pablo Counago
469. Bontcho Guentchev (in Bulgaria's 3-1 victory over Mexico during the 1994 Finals in the USA)
470. Adam Tanner

FA CUP GLORY

471. Arsenal (1-0)
472. Roger Osborne
473. Mick Mills
474. Cardiff City
475. Paul Mariner
476. Hartlepool United
477. Brian Talbot & Colin Viljoen (2)
478. Bristol Rovers
479. West Bromwich Albion
480. Arsenal Stadium (Highbury)

THE LEAGUE CUP - 1

481. John Wark (v. Blackburn Rovers)
482. John Wark (v. Liverpool)
483. Northampton Town
484. Barnsley (lost 2-0 at Portman Road in the 1st Round, 1960-1961)
485. Walsall
486. Doncaster Rovers (0-2 away in Round 2)
487. Tommy Miller & Ian Westlake (v. Brentford in Round 1)
488. George Burley
489. None
490. Leeds United (Round 2) & Bradford City (Round 3)

LEADING GOALSCORERS BY SEASON - 2

491.	1967-1968	Ray Crawford	21
492.	1971-1972	Mick Hill	8
493.	1975-1976	Trevor Whymark	15

494.	1979-1980	Paul Mariner	22
495.	1982-1983	John Wark	23
496.	1986-1987	Kevin Wilson	25
497.	1990-1991	Chris Kiwomya	12
498.	1994-1995	Claus Thomsen	5
499.	1999-2000	David Johnson	23
500.	2002-2003	Pablo Counago	20

ARNOLD MUHREN

501.	1978
502.	John Motson
503.	Liverpool (at Portman Road on 22 August 1978)
504.	214
505.	FC Twente
506.	Manchester United
507.	1982
508.	An FA Cup winners' medal with Manchester United
509.	Ajax Amsterdam
510.	6

TREVOR WHYMARK

511.	1969 (May)
512.	Colchester, Peterborough & Southend
513.	Manchester City
514.	Vancouver Whitecaps
515.	Derby County
516.	104
517.	1985
518.	1 (v. Luxembourg)
519.	2
520.	335 (includes 13 substitute appearances)

SEASON 2000-2001

521.	AZ 67 Alkmaar (Town won 2-1) & Fiorentina (Town drew 1-1)
522.	Tottenham Hotspur (on 19 August)
523.	Mark Venus (in the game in Q522)
524.	Leeds United (2-1 away on 16 September)
525.	Marcus Stewart
526.	Alun Armstrong
527.	5th
528.	Manchester City

529.   66
530.   Aston Villa

THE MANAGERS

531.	George Burley	28.12.1994	11.10.2002
532.	Bobby Robson	13.01.1969	18.08.1982
533.	Jackie Milburn	01.05.1963	08.09.1964
534.	John Lyall	11.05.1990	05.12.1994
535.	Bobby Ferguson	19.08.1982	17.05.1987
536.	A Scott Duncan	12.11.1937	07.08.1955
537.	Bill McGarry	05.10.1964	23.11.1968
538.	John Duncan	17.06.1987	05.05.1990
539.	Alf Ramsey	08.08.1955	30.04.1963
540.	Jimmy Forsyth (Caretaker)	09.09.1964	04.10.1964

TRIVIA - 6

541.   He was the first non-British player to score a goal in the FA Cup Final
        (he scored a penalty in Manchester United's 4-0 Replay win over Brighton
        & Hove Albion)
542.   22,863
543.   West Ham United
544.   Alex Mathie
545.   6th
546.   Port Vale (Town lost 4-2 at home on 23 January 1996)
547.   They qualified for the UEFA Cup (the Texaco Cup was a competition for
        teams that failed to qualify for Europe)
548.   Norwich City
549.   Blackburn Rovers
550.   Wimbledon (4-1 at home & 2-1 away)

PLAYERS - 6

551.   John Wark (for Scotland against New Zealand in Spain 1982)
552.   Ray Crawford
553.   Colin Viljoen
554.   Paul Mason
555.   Clive Woods
556.   Alec Chamberlain
557.   9
558.   Manchester City
559.   Tommy Miller
560.   Marco van Basten (v. The Soviet Union)

HIGHEST AGGREGATE SCORE IN HOME GAMES

561.	Won 11-0	Cromer (FA Cup)	31.10.1936
562.	Won 8-2	Newport County Reserves (Southern League)	16.10.1937
563.	Won 10-0	Floriana (European Cup)	25.09.1962
564.	Won 6-4	Crewe Alexandra (Division 1)	17.01.2004
565.	Won 7-2	Aldershot (Div. 3 South)	26.04.1939
566.	Won 6-3	Leyton Orient (Division 2)	02.01.1960
567.	Lost 2-7	Manchester United (Division 1)	03.09.1963
568.	Won 8-1	Avenir Beggen (UEFA Cup)	29.08.2002
569.	Won 8-0	Stowmarket (FA Cup)	03.10.1936
570.	Won 7-1	Lowestoft Town (FA Cup)	21.10.1936

SCORING DEBUTANTS - 1

571.	David Unsworth	Sheffield United
572.	Darren Currie	Queens Park Rangers
573.	Shefki Kuqi	Watford
574.	Martijn Reuser	Fulham
575.	Marcus Stewart	Barnsley
576.	Jason Dozzell	Coventry City
577.	Colin Viljoen	Portsmouth
578.	Ian Marshall	Oldham Athletic
579.	John O'Rourke	Cardiff City
580.	Ray Crawford	Swansea City

I LEFT TOWN AND JOINED CITY

581.	Geoff Hammond	Manchester City
582.	Ken Thompson	Exeter City
583.	Keith Bertschin	Birmingham City
584.	Richie Appleby	Swansea City
585.	Gary Croft	Cardiff City
586.	Louie Donowa	Bristol City
587.	John Miller	Norwich City
588.	John O'Rourke	Coventry City
589.	Neil Woods	Bradford City
590.	Bill Baxter	Hull City

SHEFKI KUQI

591.	2003 (on loan September to November, signed November)
592.	Sheffield Wednesday
593.	Stockport County
594.	£700,000

595.	MP Helsinki & HJK Helsinki
596.	Yugoslavia (on 10 November 1976)
597.	10
598.	4
599.	£300,000
600.	Hansa Rostock

SQUAD NUMBERS 2004-2005 - 2

601.	Adem Atay	No. 27
602.	Drissa Diallo	No. 5
603.	Shane Supple	No. 31
604.	Dean McDonald	No. 15
605.	Aidan Collins	No. 20
606.	Tommy Miller	No. 8
607.	Matthew Richards	No. 3
608.	Gerard Nash	No. 28
609.	Jim Magilton	No. 7
610.	Darryl Knights	No. 22

BLUES SEEING RED

611.	Fabian Wilnis
612.	Charlie George
613.	Birmingham City
614.	Drissa Diallo
615.	Georges Santos
616.	Pablo Counago (2), Hermann Hreidarsson & Chris Makin
617.	Steve McCall
618.	Terry Butcher
619.	Colin Viljoen
620.	Teddy Sheringham (winner with Manchester United in 1999)

PAUL COOPER

621.	1974 (March)
622.	Birmingham City
623.	Leicester City
624.	Leeds United (away on 20 April 1974)
625.	1987 (June)
626.	Charlton Athletic (away in the Division 1/2 Play-Off Semi-Final, 2nd Leg on 17 May 1987)
627.	680
628.	Stockport County

629.   45 (1986-1987)
630.   Manchester City (March 1989 to August 1990)

PAUL MARINER
631.   1976 (September)
632.   Chorley
633.   Manchester United (away on 30 October 1976)
634.   35
635.   Arsenal
636.   135
637.   1984 (February)
638.   Bolton (on 22 May 1953)
639.   Portsmouth
640.   Coventry City (at Portman Road on 4 February 1984)

TRIVIA - 7
641.   A swallow dive
642.   102
643.   Ajax Amsterdam
644.   72
645.   David Johnson
646.   5th
647.   Bobby Robson
648.   Brescia, Foggia, Reggiana & Salemitana
649.   Middlesbrough
650.   73

PLAYERS - 7
651.   Charlie Woods
652.   Scott Barron
653.   Marcus Stewart
654.   Eric Gates, Chris Kiwomya, Paul Mariner, Alex Mathie & Kevin Wilson
655.   Bryan Hamilton
656.   2
657.   Ajax Amsterdam
658.   Cardiff City
659.   David Johnson, Mick Lambert & Trevor Whymark
660.   NK Maribor

THE HISTORY - 2
661.   Ray Crawford (203 goals from 1958 to 1969)

662.   Allan Hunter
663.   Matteo Sereni (from Sampdoria in August 2001)
664.   Aston Villa
665.   Fulham
666.   1 (1978)
667.   The European Cup (1962-1963 Preliminary Round)
668.   Floriana
669.   M.A.S.H.
670.   3 (1960-1961, 1967-1968 & 1991-1992)

DERBY DAYS: IPSWICH TOWN v. NORWICH CITY - 2

671.   Mick Mills
672.   John Wark
673.   Paul Cooper
674.   The FA Cup (5th Round)
675.   Richard Naylor
676.   Paul Mariner
677.   Clive Woods
678.   FA, Full Members & League Cups
679.   The Norfolk & Suffolk League
680.   33 (Won: 15, Drew: 6, Lost: 12)

MON£Y MATT£RS

681.   Ron Atkinson (Manchester United)
682.   24,520
683.   Chief Executive Officer (CEO)
684.   £200,000
685.   Pioneer
686.   £15,000
687.   Arsenal
688.   1 shilling
689.   £60
690.   £3,000

THE BOSS - JOE ROYLE

691.   Everton
692.   5
693.   Manchester City
694.   The Football League Cup
695.   A bad knee injury
696.   Oldham Athletic

697. Everton
698. 1995 (Everton beat Manchester United 1-0 at Wembley)
699. 6
700. 2002 (on 28 October 2002)

COMINGS AND GOINGS - 3

701.	Brian Talbot	to Arsenal
702.	Jimmy Robertson	from Arsenal
703.	Micky Stockwell	to Colchester United
704.	Matteo Sereni	from Sampdoria
705.	Alan Sunderland	to Derry City
706.	Romeo Zondervan	from West Bromwich Albion
707.	Eddie Youds	to Bradford City
708.	Trevor Whymark	from Diss Town
709.	Colin Viljoen	to Manchester City
710.	Clive Woods	to Norwich City

THE 1980s - 2

711. 1980-1981 & 1981-1982
712. Frans Thijssen
713. Terry Butcher
714. Colchester United
715. Manchester United & Leeds United
716. Mick Mills
717. Paul Mariner
718. 6
719. John Wark
720. An Electronic Scoreboard

ALAN BRAZIL

721. 1977 (May)
722. Manchester United (at Old Trafford on 14 January 1978)
723. 212 (includes 18 as substitute)
724. Tottenham Hotspur
725. 1983 (March)
726. 13 (11 whilst he was with Town)
727. Manchester United
728. Coventry City
729. Talksport
730. 1981-1982 (28 goals)

MICK MILLS - 2

731. Paul Mariner
732. 25
733. The Second Division Championship in 1968
734. 1972 (on 11 October v. Yugoslavia)
735. None
736. 1978
737. 1982 (after the World Cup Finals)
738. 5
739. 8
740. Ipswich Town

UEFA CUP WINNERS - 2

741. Widzew Lodz
742. Paul Mariner
743. FC Cologne
744. Tony Woodcock
745. Johnny Rep
746. John Wark (a 13th-minute penalty against Aris Salonika in the 1st Round, 1st Leg)
747. Bohemians Prague
748. FC Cologne & St Etienne
749. Paul Mariner, Frans Thijssen & John Wark
750. Bohemians Prague & Widzew Lodz

TRIVIA - 8

751. Belgium
752. Lewis Price
753. None
754. Liverpool (3rd) & Leeds United (4th)
755. 57
756. Ipswich Town (23 goals), (Everton 7 & Leicester City 10)
757. 17th
758. George Burley (1995-1996)
759. 1995
760. 119

PLAYERS - 8

761. David Unsworth (v. Sheffield United, Coca-Cola Championship)
762. 12
763. Ipswich (Rugby) Football Club

764. David Johnson
765. 46 (including 3 as substitute)
766. Fabian Wilnis
767. Paul Mariner (for England against France during the 1982 Finals in Spain)
768. Tony Mowbray
769. Darren Bent
770. A European Championships winners' medal with Holland

SIR ALF RAMSEY - 2

771. Walter Winterbottom
772. 1961
773. 1955-1956 & 1956-1957 (25 wins)
774. 29 (Won: 13, Drew: 4, Lost: 12)
775. Burnley (2-1 home win on 27th April 1963)
776. 1974 (on 19 April)
777. 340
778. 1999
779. The British Home International Championships (includes 3 shared)
780. Jimmy Adamson

BLUES' PLAYER OF THE YEAR - 3

781. 2001-02   Mark Venus
782. 1998-99   Jamie Clapham
783. 1995-96   Simon Milton
784. 1993-94   John Wark
785. 1990-91   David Linighan
786. 1982-83   Paul Mariner
787. 1981-82   Alan Brazil
788. 1979-80   Frans Thijssen
789. 1977-78   Mick Mills
790. 1974-75   Colin Viljoen

FRANS THIJSSEN

791. Dutch
792. 1979 (February)
793. FC Twente
794. Arnold Muhren (his teammate at FC Twente)
795. Brian Talbot
796. Derby County (away on 28 February 1979, First Division)
797. 1983
798. Vancouver Whitecaps

799.   Nottingham Forest
800.   3

SEASON 2003-2004 - 2

801.   Crystal Palace (Play-Off winners)
802.   21 (12 at home & 9 away)
803.   Southend United (4-2), Colchester United (3-0) & Boston United (2-0)
804.   They all began with the letter "W" (Wigan, West Bromwich Albion, West Ham United, Walsall, Wimbledon & Watford)
805.   Derby County
806.   Shefki Kuqi (in a 1-1 draw at home on the final day of the season)
807.   Darren Bent (1-0 home win on 15 May 2004)
808.   Norwich City, West Bromwich Albion, Sunderland & West Ham United
809.   Pablo Counago, Shefki Kuqi & Tommy Miller
810.   Darren Bent

FIRST DIVISION CHAMPIONS

811.   1961-1962
812.   Alf Ramsey
813.   Burnley
814.   56
815.   24 (Won: 24, Drew: 8, Lost: 10)
816.   Fulham (2-4 on 23rd September 1961)
817.   Ray Crawford
818.   33
819.   Norwich City (1-2 in a 4th Round Replay at Portman Road)
820.   Tottenham Hotspur (Double winners in 1960-1961)

SEASON 2004-2005 - 2

821.   Oxford United
822.   Queens Park Rangers & Watford
823.   Shefki Kuqi
824.   Coventry City (on 15 January 2005 at Portman Road)
825.   Coventry City
826.   Nottingham Forest
827.   Darren Bent & Jim Magilton
828.   Tommy Miller (in Town's 3-1 defeat in the 3rd Round to Bolton Wanderers)
829.   Leicester City & Watford
830.   Ian Westlake (on 21 August 2004)

ALL-TIME LEADING GOAL SCORERS - 1

831.	Matt Holland	45
832.	Bryan Hamilton	56
833.	Alex Mathie	47
834.	John Wark	179
835.	Eric Gates	96
836.	Alan Brazil	80
837.	Tommy Parker	92
838.	Chris Kiwomya	64
839.	Kevin Wilson	49
840.	Tom Garneys	143

TRIVIA - 9

841.	Sheffield Wednesday
842.	Oxford United
843.	Leicester City, Tranmere Rovers, Wigan Athletic, Swindon Town & Norwich City
844.	8 (Won: 2, Drew: 2, Lost: 4)
845.	Ray Crawford
846.	The Dogs of War
847.	Paul Gascoigne
848.	32
849.	Crewe Alexandra
850.	Shefki Kuqi & Tommy Miller

PLAYERS - 9

851.	Paul Mariner (12)
852.	Mick Mills (40), Matt Holland (10), Andy Nelson (3), Allan Hunter (3), Paul Mariner (2), Ken Malcolm (1), Brian Talbot (1), Jamie Clapham (1) & John McGreal (1)
853.	Frank Clarke
854.	Clive Baker
855.	Brian Talbot (with Town when they beat Arsenal, and with Arsenal when they beat Manchester United)
856.	Matt Richards
857.	Laurie Sivell
858.	John Wark (v. Aris Salonika, 1st Round, 1st Leg)
859.	Tony Vaughan
860.	Terry Butcher (1982 & 1986 when he was at Town and 1990 when he was at Glasgow Rangers)

THE 1970s - 2

861.   1973-1974 (19 goals)
862.   The Portman Stand
863.   Manchester United (31,918 watched Town win 4-1) & Arsenal (34,636 saw a 2-1 loss)
864.   Real Madrid & SS Lazio
865.   Liverpool
866.   Arnold Muhren
867.   Millwall (Town won the 6th Round tie 6-1 at The Den)
868.   Paul Mariner (from Plymouth Argyle)
869.   4th
870.   Nottingham Forest

MICK STOCKWELL

871.   1985 (on 26 December)
872.   Colchester United
873.   611 (includes 53 as substitute)
874.   2000 (July)
875.   None
876.   Heybridge Swifts
877.   10
878.   Coventry City (away on Boxing Day 1985)
879.   Stockport County (away in Division 1 on 15 April 2000)
880.   Woodbridge Town

TOWN IN EUROPE - 2

881.   Barcelona
882.   AZ 67 Alkmaar (1st Round of the 1978-1979 ECWC & the 1980-1981 UEFA Cup Final)
883.   86
884.   Kevin O'Callaghan (7)
885.   Paul Cooper (34)
886.   120 (119 by Town players & 1 own goal)
887.   25
888.   Trevor Whymark (13)
889.   6 (season 1978-1979)
890.   1973-1974

ERIC GATES

891. 1972 (October)
892. Wolverhampton Wanderers (at Portman Road in the First Division on 27 October 1973)
893. 2
894. Sunderland
895. 101
896. 1985 (August)
897. Ron Greenwood
898. Carlisle United
899. West Ham United
900. 417 (includes 39 as substitute)

FULL MEMBERS CUP - 2

901. 1991-1992
902. English clubs were re-admitted to the 3 major European competitions
903. 3 (Bobby Ferguson, John Duncan & John Lyall)
904. Chris Kiwomya (on 26 November 1991 away v. Chelsea in a 2-2 draw)
905. Blackburn Rovers
906. Chelsea & Wimbledon
907. Nigel Gleghorn
908. Chelsea (1989-90 & 1991-92)
909. John Wark (2), Mich D'Avray, John Deehan & David Lowe
910. Norwich City

IPSWICH IN THE FA CUP - 2

911. Manchester City
912. Paul Mason (v. Walsall & Aston Villa)
913. Mick Mills
914. Nottingham Forest
915. Bradford City
916. Tony Humes
917. Sheffield United (3rd Round) & Manchester United (4th Round)
918. Southampton
919. 5 (Round 1 plus 2 Replays & Round 2 plus a Replay)
920. Leeds United

FINAL LEAGUE POSITIONS - 3

921.	1967-1968	Div 2	1st
922.	1974-1975	Div 1	3rd
923.	1979-1980	Div 1	3rd

924.	1981-1982	Div 1	2nd
925.	1988-1989	Div 2	8th
926.	1993-1994	Prem	19th
927.	1994-1995	Prem	22nd
928.	1996-1997	Div 1	4th
929.	2000-2001	Prem	5th
930.	2001-2002	Prem	18th

THE LEAGUE CUP - 2

931. Liverpool
932. Alex Mathie & Mauricio Taricco
933. David Johnson
934. John Wark (12 goals)
935. Alf Ramsey (1960-1961)
936. Kevin Steggles
937. Alan Brazil & Eric Gates
938. Steve Sedgley
939. Mick Stockwell
940. 148

TRIVIA - 10

941. Birmingham City
942. Austria (on 4 April 1962)
943. 2001
944. Millwall
945. John Lyall
946. TSV Alemannia Aachen
947. Newcastle United, Norwich City & Wolverhampton Wanderers
948. Tunbridge Wells Rangers
949. 6 (12 October 1991 to 2 November 1991)
950. 1976

PLAYERS - 10

951. Eddie Youds & Frank Yallop
952. Ray Crawford
953. Crystal Palace
954. Bobby Petta
955. Trevor Putney
956. NAC Breda
957. Mick Mills
958. Colchester United (February 1981)

959.   Sam Parkin
960.   Queens Park Rangers

LEADING GOALSCORERS BY SEASON - 3

961.	1969-1970	Colin Viljoen	6
962.	1973-1974	Bryan Hamilton	19
963.	1976-1977	Trevor Whymark	15
964.	1977-1978	Paul Mariner	22
965.	1980-1981	John Wark	36
966.	1983-1984	Eric Gates	16
967.	1985-1986	Kevin Wilson	15
968.	1991-1992	Chris Kiwomya	19
969.	1993-1994	Ian Marshall	15
970.	2000-2001	Marcus Stewart	21

SCORING DEBUTANTS - 2

971.	Neil Midgley	West Bromwich Albion
972.	Gary Croft	Manchester City
973.	Kevin Wilson	Gillingham
974.	Paul Mason	Oldham Athletic
975.	David Johnson	Wolverhampton Wanderers
976.	Alex Mathie	Southampton
977.	Adam Tanner	Leicester City
978.	Mark Stuart	Watford
979.	Sergei Baltacha	Stoke City
980.	Keith Bertschin	Arsenal

RAY CRAWFORD

981.   1958 (September)
982.   Portsmouth (December 1954 to September 1958)
983.   Swansea City (away in Division 2 on 4 October 1958)
984.   2
985.   Wolverhampton Wanderers
986.   40
987.   1963 (September)
988.   Colchester United
989.   Charlton Athletic
990.   Wolverhampton Wanderers (away in Division 1 on 1 March 1969)

JOHN WARK - 2

991.   1988 (January)

992. 25
993. 18
994. Middlesbrough (August 1991)
995. Joe Fagan
996. £450,000
997. The Professional Footballers' Association Player of the Year Award
998. Watford
999. 2 (with Liverpool in 1983-84 & 1985-86)
1000. Paul Goddard

MARCUS BENT

1001. 2001 (November)
1002. Blackburn Rovers
1003. Middlesbrough (away on 25 November 2001)
1004. £3 million
1005. Leicester City
1006. 23
1007. Everton
1008. £450,000
1009. Brentford
1010. Sheffield United

UNLUCKY KEEPERS

1011. Kelvin Davis
1012. Lewis Price
1013. Craig Forrest
1014. Matteo Sereni
1015. Matt Holland
1016. Huddersfield Town
1017. Marcus Stewart
1018. Jack Parry
1019. Paul Cooper
1020. Clive Baker

JOHN LYALL

1021. 1990 (11 May)
1022. West Ham United
1023. Sheffield Wednesday (lost 0-2 at home on 25 August 1990 in Division 2)
1024. 15 (1974-1989)
1025. 2 (with West Ham United)
1026. 1975 & 1980

1027. 3rd (West Ham United)
1028. 1985-1986
1029. The Second Division Championship
1030. 1992

SEASON 1981-1982

1031. Glasgow Rangers
1032. Sunderland
1033. Vasco da Gama
1034. Aberdeen (1-3 at Pittodrie in the UEFA Cup 1st Round, 2nd Leg)
1035. Alan Brazil
1036. Eric Gates
1037. Liverpool
1038. Tottenham Hotspur
1039. 87 (3 points for a win system was introduced)
1040. 4 (Liverpool had 91 points)

IPSWICH TOWN v. MANCHESTER UNITED - 2

1041. George Burley (1997 League Cup 3rd Round, 2-0 win at Portman Road)
1042. Alex Mathie & Mauricio Taricco
1043. 67,597 (on 23 December 2000 at Old Trafford)
1044. John Wark
1045. 56 (Won: 19, Drew: 9, Lost: 28)
1046. John Wark (at Portman Road on 20 April 1982 in Division 1)
1047. Alan Brazil
1048. Paul Mariner
1049. Gary Bailey
1050. Ted Phillips

ALL-TIME LEADING GOALSCORERS - 2

1051. Paul Mariner   135
1052. David Johnson   62
1053. Ted Phillips   179
1054. Jason Dozzell   73
1055. Trevor Whymark   104
1056. Gerard Baker   66
1057. Colin Viljoen   54
1058. Mick Lambert   45
1059. Simon Milton   56
1060. Frank Brogan   69

KEVIN BEATTIE

1061. 1971 (July)
1062. Manchester United (away in Division 1 on 12 August 1972)
1063. 321 (includes 11 as substitute)
1064. Colchester United
1065. 1982 (July)
1066. 9
1067. 1975 (on 16 April)
1068. Malcolm MacDonald (Newcastle United)
1069. Scotland (on 24 May 1975 in a 5-1 win at Wembley)
1070. The Beat

DAVID JOHNSON

1071. 1972 (November)
1072. Everton
1073. 9
1074. Liverpool
1075. 46
1076. 1976 (August)
1077. Manchester City
1078. Tulsa Roughnecks
1079. Leeds United (at Portman Road on 4 November 1972)
1080. 178 (includes 4 as substitute)

TED PHILLIPS

1081. 1953 (December)
1082. Luton Town (February to September 1965)
1083. Watford (away in Division 3 South on 3 March 1954)
1084. A Scott Duncan
1085. Colchester United
1086. 295
1087. 1
1088. Bricklaying
1089. Leyton Orient
1090. 181

TOWN AT WEMBLEY

1091. 4
1092. 1928
1093. Southern Amateur League (Ealing were granted permission to play their
       home games at Wembley Stadium due to drainage problems at their own

ground)
1094. Arsenal (1978)
1095. Nottingham Forest (1978)
1096. 2000
1097. Barnsley (Division 1 Play-Off Final)
1098. Martijn Reuser (against Barnsley in the 2000 Division 1 Play-Off Final: Tony Mowbray, Richard Naylor & Marcus Stewart also scored)
1099. 42
1100. Mick Mills (in the 1978 FA Cup Final & 1978 FA Charity Shield)

TOWN AT THE MOVIES
1101. Escape to Victory
1102. 5
1103. Kevin O'Callaghan, Russell Osman, Laurie Sivell, Robin Turner & John Wark (Sivell & Turner played for Germany in the movie)
1104. Kazimierz Deyna & Mike Summerbee
1105. Yesterday's Hero
1106. Joan Collins & Ian McShane
1107. Bobby Moore & Pele
1108. Michael Caine
1109. Sylvester Stallone
1110. Osvaldo Ardiles

ALLAN HUNTER
1111. 1971 (September)
1112. Blackburn Rovers
1113. Coleraine
1114. 53 (47 times with Town)
1115. 1982 (May)
1116. 10
1117. Leicester City (at Portman Road in Division 1 on 11 September 1971)
1118. Shrewsbury Town (away in an FA Cup 5th Round tie on 13 February 1982)
1119. Oldham Athletic (January 1967 to June 1969)
1120. Colchester United

THE 1990s
1121. John Lyall
1122. 3-1 at home & 2-0 at Carrow Road (season 1992-1993)
1123. Wrexham
1124. Millwall

1125. Kieron Dyer (to Newcastle United)
1126. George Burley
1127. 1993-1994
1128. Oxford United
1129. John Wark
1130. Charlton Athletic

JOHN DUNCAN

1131. 1987 (17 June)
1132. Aston Villa (at Portman Road on 15 August in a 1-1 draw, Division 2)
1133. 1990
1134. West Bromwich Albion (away on 5 May, 3-1 win, Division 2)
1135. Dundee
1136. Tottenham Hotspur
1137. £160,000
1138. Derby County
1139. Scunthorpe United
1140. Chesterfield

MIXED BAG

1141. Bill Werbeniuk (who sadly passed away in January 2003)
1142. Norwich City
1143. 28 (14 October 1950 to 26 March 1951)
1144. Wigan Athletic (away in the Nationwide League Division 1 on 26 August 2003)
1145. Manchester City (on 3 December 1994, a 1-2 home loss in the FA Premier League)
1146. Barcelona (European Cup Winners' Cup)
1147. Darren Bent
1148. Ray Crawford
1149. 91
1150. David Johnson

JIM MAGILTON

1151. 1999 (on 17 January)
1152. Sheffield Wednesday
1153. Liverpool (May 1986 to October 1990)
1154. Oxford United
1155. Belfast (on 6 May 1969)
1156. Southampton
1157. £1.6 million

1158.   Sunderland (away on 17 January 1999 in Division 1)
1159.   Season 1999-2000
1160.   £682,500

GEORGE BURLEY

1161.   1973 (Youth Team)
1162.   Sunderland
1163.   Manchester United (on 29 December 1973)
1164.   Gillingham
1165.   11
1166.   1994
1167.   Derby County
1168.   2000
1169.   1982-1983
1170.   Colchester United

THE 1960's

1171.   1966
1172.   Colin Viljoen
1173.   Ray Crawford
1174.   The Second Division Championship
1175.   Leeds United
1176.   1964-1965
1177.   Wolverhampton Wanderers
1178.   1967-1968
1179.   Norwich City
1180.   Gerry Baker

SIMON MILTON

1181.   1987 (July)
1182.   None, he retired
1183.   329 (includes 71 as substitute)
1184.   Bury Town
1185.   £5,500
1186.   Torquay United
1187.   1998
1188.   56
1189.   He decided to retire
1190.   Northampton Town (at Portman Road in the League Cup 2nd Round, 1st
        Leg on 22nd September 1987)

UP FOR THE CUP

1191. Chelsea (in the 3rd Round, 0-3 at Stamford Bridge)
1192. Tottenham Hotspur
1193. Manchester City
1194. Mark Brennan, Tony Humes & Kevin Wilson
1195. 3 (Newcastle United, WBA & Stoke City)
1196. The Ipswich Hospital Cup
1197. Alun Armstrong, Marcus Stewart & Jermaine Wright
1198. Wolverhampton Wanderers (0-1 away in a 4th Round Replay)
1199. West Bromwich Albion
1200. Grasshoppers Zurich